Thinking Straight

Thinking
Straight

*A systematic guide to managerial
problem-solving and decision-making that works*

Steve Kneeland

PATHWAYS

Also available in abridged form as *Effective Problem Solving*,
by Steve Kneeland, published by How To Books in 1998.

First published in 1999 by
How To Books Ltd., 3 Newtec Place,
Magdalen Road, Oxford OX4 1RE, United Kingdom
Tel: 01865 793806   Fax: 01865 248780

British Library Cataloguing in Publication Data
A catalogue record for this book is available from
the British Library

Editing by Dave Venner   Cover image PhotoDisc
Cover design by Shireen Nathoo Design

Produced for How To Books by Deer Park Productions
Typeset by Euroset, Alresford, Hampshire SO24 9PQ
Printed and bound in Great Britain.

Note: The material contained in this book is set out in good
faith for general guidance and no liability can be accepted for
loss or expense incurred as a result of relying in particular
circumstances on statements made in the book. The laws and
regulations are complex and liable to change, and readers
should check the current position with the relevant
authorities before making personal arrangements.

Pathways is an imprint of
How To Books

Contents

List of Illustrations

Preface

I am confident that, when you finish reading this book, you will be a more effective problem-solver.

I say that because I am now writing the preface. The preface is the part of the book I decided to do last, and it won't get done until I am satisfied with the rest of the book. And being satisfied means being confident that, when you finish reading this book, you the reader will be a more effective problem-solver. Hence my opening statement.

A book – any book – is a collaborative effort. I have to acknowledge the encouragement, patience, support, and businesslike assistance of Giles Lewis and Nikki Read. This book, hopefully, will be just one of many joint efforts to provide you – the business reader – with things that are honestly and truly worth reading.

On the home front, Pam and the kids – Jessica and Jennifer – have somehow resisted the temptation to throw both me and my computer into the duck pond that sits behind our house, and without their support and understanding this book … could probably have been finished a lot sooner. But it wouldn't, I am sure, have been as good.

You, the reader, will have the final word. Use the book. Think of it as a tool. Something to be not just read but thought about, scribbled on, fiddled with, and hopefully added in a helpful fashion to your already-existing storehouse of knowledge and insight. Will it actually make you a more effective problem-solver? Yes, I think it will.

Steve Kneeland

Take
something
you're pretty
good at and
become better

CHAPTER 1

An Overview of What Lies Ahead

O ur aim in this chapter is to take the overview and look at our total problem-solving 'system'. Then, starting in the next chapter, we'll get into the details.

Books are built around assumptions, and it's probably wise to get them out on the table as early as possible.

Assumption 1 is that we want to maximise your effectiveness as a problem-solver.

Assumption 2 is that we're not starting from scratch. This is not a book for people who don't know how to solve problems.

Assumption 3 is that you're aware of the importance of thinking straight. Getting things in the right order. Being systematic.

These three assumptions, hopefully, will set the tone for the book as a whole. Quantitative tools – decision matrices and the like – will be touched upon only briefly. Brainstorming will not be given a lengthy treatment because we don't see too many managers using it as a problem-solving tool. Anything that won't help make you a more effective problem-solver will be left out.

Remember to be pragmatic

What we *will* emphasise, on the other hand, are the pragmatics of problem-solving. *The things that make a difference in real life business situations.*

- ◆ Managing a crisis situation.
- ◆ Thinking strategically.
- ◆ Weighing the risks.
- ◆ Exercising business judgement.
- ◆ Trusting your instincts.
- ◆ Rallying support for a solution.

♦ Selling your ideas.
♦ Getting the whole team involved.

We'll start – in this chapter – with an overview of what lies ahead. The first item on the agenda is a conceptual model of the total problem-solving process.

The AIDOSE model

What's the single most important thing that we can do to become more effective problem-solvers?

The answer is – beg, borrow, steal, or develop a step-by-step model of the problem-solving process and start using it. Consistently. Day in and day out. Until it becomes second nature.

The six-step model that we will be using is shown in Figure 1, and we will be looking at it in more detail in the next chapter. For now, there are just two or three key points to be made:

♦ There is no right or wrong model. What counts is that a model helps us operate more effectively.
♦ The trick is to find a model that works for us … that suits the way we do things anyway.
♦ And then – stick with it and use it consistently, so that it becomes an integral part of how we think.

Chapters 3 through 8, will focus one by one on each of the six

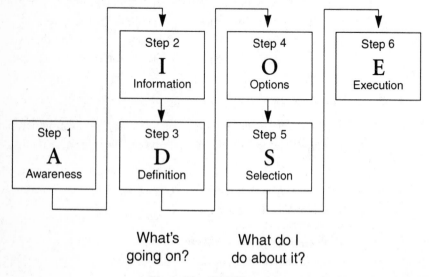

Fig. 1. The AIDOSE model.

steps in our problem-solving model. Our aim in each of these chapters will be to:

- Establish clearly the *rationale* for the step.
- Bring that phase of the model to *life*, make it *real*.
- Introduce whatever 'techniques' might be helpful.
- Examine some of the pitfalls we have to watch for.

For now, let's content ourselves with taking the overview and getting a feel for how the model works on a fairly general level.

Step 1 – A for awareness

We've got a problem. That's Step 1 – the *awareness* stage. We are aware that we have a problem to solve, but, as of yet, there has been no information-gathering. Immediately, however – and this is the essence of our work in Step 1 – There is a preliminary assessment. We ask four questions (Figure 2):

- What – exactly – is the problem?
- How urgent is it?
- How important is it?
- Whose responsibility is it?

We are dealing with the problem as it has presented itself. We are simply reacting to and trying to make sense of whatever information is there.

In Chapter 3, we will examine these four questions in more detail. Asking them will become a routine, permanent part of our problem-solving 'system'.

Our goal

Every chapter of this book will have a goal. The goal of Chapter 3 – the *awareness* chapter – is that you become aware of problems earlier than other people do.

> Word will get around that you have an unusual knack for sensing that a problem exists before it actually jumps out of the bushes. You have your antenna up.

You are sensitive to the environment. It is not often that you are caught unaware or off-guard. You can generally spot a problem early on.

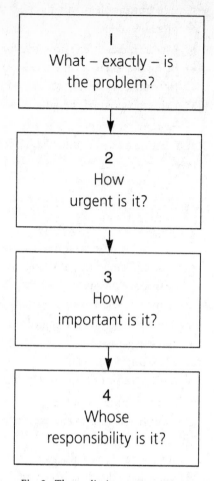

Fig. 2. The preliminary assessment.

By the time we get to the end of Chapter 3, that's what we want people to be saying about you.

Step 2 – I for information

Okay, I've decided to solve the problem. Now I need to find out more about it. That moves us into Step 2.

The gathering of information doesn't have to be done in a formal, structured fashion. More often than not, it simply means thinking about the problem, observing, perhaps raising the issue in a meeting. *Talking* to people is still the best source of information about a problem, especially in the early stages when we are trying to get an initial 'fix' on the problem.

Even 'technical' information is best relayed by someone who can communicate the subtleties, the question marks, the things which they sense are there but haven't shown up clearly in the data or the X-ray.

So, when we get to Chapter 4 – which is where we deal with information-gathering in some depth – our emphasis will be on seeing for ourselves what is going on and asking the right questions:

- *What* has happened, and precisely how did it happen?
- *Where* and *when* did the problem occur?
- *Who* are the people involved, and in what way has their involvement affected the situation?
- *Why* hasn't the situation resolved itself?

Step 3 – D for definition

A problem, we have said, is a *gap* between the way things are and the way they ought to be. We *define* a problem by placing all the information we have into one of four boxes, two on each side of the gap (Figure 3).

The S (symptoms) and C (causes) boxes on the left have to do with the way things are right now, while the O (outcomes) and C (constraints) boxes on the right have to do with the way we would *like* things to be once we've solved the problem.

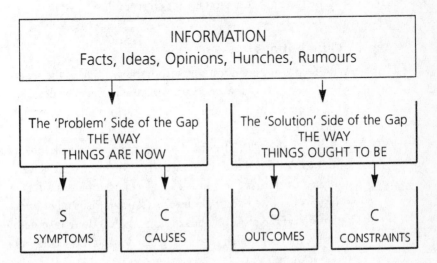

Fig. 3. Defining the problem.

All that sounds simple enough, but the challenge of actually doing it can be enormous. Understanding the problem means much more than simply gathering the facts and arranging them in a way that makes sense. Defining the problem means *thinking* about those facts.

And then on to action

Steps 2, the gathering of information, and 3, definition of the problem, are closely intertwined.

As we gather information, we are working to define and understand the problem. The two processes – even though we represent them as separate steps in our model – go on simultaneously. We gather information about the problem. We think about it, chew on it, add it to what we already have. We're *building* an understanding of the problem.

And, once it's built to our satisfaction – once we sense that we understand what the problem is all about – we stop.

So Step 2 can be a long one. Step 3, on the other hand, is where we end up at the end of Step 2. We've defined the problem.

Let's repeat those three conditions. We have defined the problem when:

- We understand what the problem is all about it.
- We feel comfortable taking action to solve it.
- The time has come to take action regardless.

Step 4 – O for options

With Step 4 our attention shifts from the *problem* to the *solution* – from investigating and understanding the problem to deciding what to do about it. To identifying the various *solutions* or options available to us.

Beware of pitfalls. The one that managers often walk into is that of not exploring all the alternatives. For whatever reason, we confine our thinking to a much smaller range of alternative solutions than we have to. Indeed, we'll often focus all of our attention on the most obvious option – unless there is something wrong with it, in which case we'll take a look at the second most obvious option.

Step 5 – S for selection

This is the point of management decision-making. All the facts are in, the problem has been identified and analysed, we've tested out a number of viable solutions … all that remains now is to make the final decision.

One might assume that the act of making a decision might have something of the 'scientific' about it. Surely, it ought to be an orderly, logical process based on a thorough consideration of the facts and the application of intelligent reasoning thereto.

In practise, it doesn't work that way. Studies of the decision-making process have shown that executives rarely have time to consider all the facts or take a rational or logical approach to making decisions in the first place. There is a marked tendency to stick with what works rather than to seek out new or unproven ideas. There is also a tendency to deliberate through face-to-face discussion rather than through a systematic reading of proposals or analysis of data. To weigh decision options in terms of whose support can be counted on and what resistance or opposition will likely be encountered.

So – as will be the case throughout the book – we will try to be very realistic and pragmatic about things when we get to Chapter 7, our chapter on making a decision regarding the best solution. We won't let the computer do our thinking for us. We won't even apologise for not being entirely 'rational' in the way we go about making our decision.

Step 6 – E for execution

These days, not many important tasks are accomplished by individuals acting in isolation. In most problem-solving situations, the action required to solve the problem will involve the co-ordinated efforts of a number of different people.

Our challenge is to plan out what has to be done, get the right people together and manage their combined efforts.

All too often, this is where an otherwise good solution begins to come unglued. If we want to point a finger it's easy enough to find targets – too many people involved, too little time, not enough money, too many things going on at once …

But what we really have to look at is our own *project management* skills and know-how. There is no getting around the

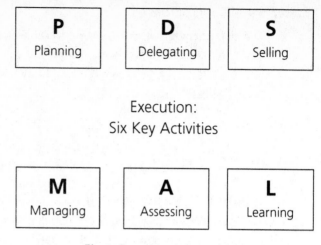

Fig. 4. Execution: six key activities.

fact that we are responsible for the successful implementation of the solution no matter how many other people might be involved. A comprehensive course on project management is not what this book is all about but we will certainly touch upon the six key areas shown in Figure 4.

Close-ups

In the final part of our book we will take a close-up look at certain important aspects of the total problem-solving cycle. Firstly, in Chapters 9 to 12, we'll turn our attention to some qualities that set the truly effective problem-solver apart from the crowd:

- ◆ Creativity.
- ◆ Intuition.
- ◆ Judgement.
- ◆ Strategic thinking.
- ◆ The ability to effectively *sell* one's solutions.

In terms of the classic distinction between the rational or left-brain side of things and the holistic or right-brain side, Chapters 9 through 12 clearly focus on the latter. Then, in our final two chapters, we will examine the whole problem-solving cycle from the vantage point of (1) the managerial role and (2) the wider organisational context. What we are doing here is blending in two crucial ingredients – *Leverage* and *Climate* – without which even the most talented and determined of problem-solvers will be handicapped.

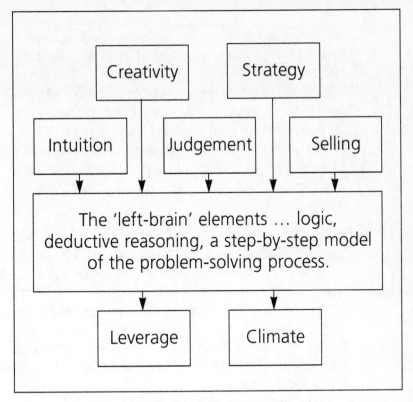

Fig.5. The total problem solver.

Add the right-brain elements of creativity, strategic thinking, intuition, business judgement, and selling ability to the left-brain logic and structure captured in our six-step model – and blend in the adroit use of managerial *leverage* and the creation of a favourable problem-solving *climate* – and the result is a total problem-solving system (Figure 5).

Our Yellow Highlighter

As a strategy for learning a yellow highlighter highlights the salient points so that they stick in the memory. By and large, there are four things we can do as a means of committing something to memory (Figure 6). Doing all four is better than doing just one,

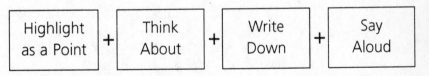

Fig. 6. Strategy for learning.

or two, or three. That is one of the very basic principles of learning; the more actively engaged we are in the process, the better we learn.

We've highlighted key points in each chapter by setting them apart in boxes. This isn't quite the same as using a yellow highlighter, but it serves the same purpose. It extracts the essence, identifies the key points, separates them from their context. We have also gathered key points together at the end of each chapter in the form of summaries.

Our 'Famous Five'

There are, hopefully, some good points to be made during the course of this book. Some genuinely useful insights to be passed along.

Where do they come from? On some occasions, the source is an expert of some standing – a Stephen Covey, for example, or a Lord Thomson, or someone who has written a classic article for the *Harvard Business Review*. Where appropriate, these sources have been duly acknowledged.

By and large, however, this book is built upon insights gleaned from managers like yourself, dealing with real issues and real problems. To capture something of the flavour of how real managers think, we have opted to include actual quotations throughout the book. At times, we are reporting what a manager once said to us, trying to remember the exact words as best we can. At other times, the quotation is part-real and part-invented … a composite, representing a point that a *lot* of different managers have made.

To help things flow smoothly, we will ascribe these quotations to a group of five fictitious managers whom we will call the *Famous Five*.

- ◆ Jennifer Adair: Customer Service Manager with a London-based tour operator.
- ◆ Jack Carter: Director of the office supplies and medical products division for a large manufacturer of industrial products.
- ◆ Tony Martindale: Director of Sales and Marketing for a leading packaged food company.

- Jill Pritchard: Columnist and author, working out of her home in Chipping Norton.
- Graeme Weir: Manufacturing director for a Leamington-based producer of automotive components.

Try to imagine these five individuals working along with us, as consultants and commentators. Five experienced and perceptive managers who all have – as we shall see – some very useful insights to offer.

*Asking the right
questions in the
right order.
Getting the
process right.*

CHAPTER 2

A Problem-Solving Model

A model that helps us think straight. A practical, usable model of the problem-solving process. That is what we will be developing in this chapter.

Problem-solving ability isn't about *intelligence*. It's not about being *smart*.

It's about *thinking straight*.

It's about *getting the process right*.

When you pay a mechanic to cure what's making that funny noise under the bonnet of your car you probably don't spent too much time worrying about how *intelligent* they are. What you worry about is whether they have the right training and the right tools to tackle the problem in a logical, step-by-step manner. To sift through a few hypotheses before settling on one that probably applies. To *test* the hypothesis carefully by taking a few tentative steps and seeing what sort of impact it makes.

Thinking straight. Asking the right questions in the right order. *Getting the process right.* That's our aim in this second chapter. What we're going to do in the next few pages is build a *model* of the problem-solving process. Whether it's a mechanic working under the bonnet of our car or someone at the Bank of England deciding whether to raise interest rates by a quarter of a point this Thursday morning, all we can ever hope for is that the person has mastered the art of straight thinking. What we want to construct here is a model which, if we apply it diligently, will more or less guarantee that this is what happens.

What is a problem?

What, exactly, is a problem? Let's start by asking that very basic question.

A problem is basically a deviation from the norm, serious enough to require correction. There is a gap between the way things are and the way we'd like them to be.

Problem-solving is the process we use to bring these two elements back into alignment. It's how we close the gap.

That's the formal definition and it's the one we'll be using in this book. But let's recognise that the word 'problem' is a very general one. We might talk, for example, about the *problem* of unemployment in the North, or about Bill's drinking *problem*, or about not having a *problem* with the idea of a stranger joining us at our table in a crowded lunchtime pub.

So we should be a bit more definitive about the sort of 'problems' we'll be covering in this book. Basically, we're situating you in a mid-level management role. And we're assuming further that a situation has come to or been brought to your attention.

- The problem concerns you as a manager. Either the variance has been brought to your attention by your superior or you sense that something is wrong – or will become wrong – and needs to be fixed.
- There is uncertainty or doubt involved in the situation. We're not sure what's causing the gap or what should be done to close it.
- Something is pressing for a solution. It can't be left as it is.

The problem might be something as simple as a proposal that has been rejected and needs a re-think or it might be something quite complex. Should our company be competing in a specific industry outside what has historically been its core business? It might be an *urgent* problem. Our supply of 6mm coil is stuck somewhere on the M25. Or, it might be something which, though perhaps important, isn't exactly crying out for attention. People in the shipping and receiving area seem to be fast losing what little respect they had for Geoff Parker, the new manager we brought in last month.

The problem might be sharply defined, with clear-cut boundaries. Bill can't make the Tuesday meeting, and he is the one who was going to do the presentation on distribution costs. Or, it might be fuzzy and amorphous, hard to get a handle on. There's not enough critical thinking around here; not enough people willing to break with tradition and challenge the status quo.

Two types of problem

To help impose some sort of order on this wide array of goings-on, let's divide the world into two parts. There are, in very broad strokes, two main types of problem that we will find ourselves dealing with. The distinction between them isn't a crucial one, and it may become rather grey-ish at times; but it will prove helpful.

1. The Fix-It problem

A *Fix-It* problem is something that needs fixing. There's something wrong with the current state of affairs and we need to find a way to change it.

- Profit contribution from our northwest region is running ten per cent behind forecast.
- We had only five complaints from January through May and all of a sudden we've got three in one week.
- The number of referrals has risen to the point where we just can't handle them all with our current set-up.
- Turnover on our sales team has hit the 20 per cent mark. The industry standard is about 10 per cent.
- Readership is down by just over 23,000 – while the *Times* and *Guardian* have both moved ahead.

In cases such as these, the fact that we've got a *problem* is quite obvious. The *gap* is clearly defined for us; it's a simple difference between what the meter *should* read and what it *does* read.

> A *Fix-It* problem is something that needs fixing. Something is wrong with the current state of affairs and we need to find a way to change it.

At other times – and this is perhaps, for someone in a managerial role at least, the more common situation – something is bothering us. It's still a *Fix-It* problem, but it's nothing so clear-cut and unambiguous as a *meter* reading.

- I think the product line as a whole is showing its age. If we don't do something soon, we're dead.
- I don't like the way my daughter is behaving. I think she's getting it from school.

- Your proposal contains some sound ideas, John, but there's not enough *excitement* in it.
- I'm not happy with the way Jim is performing. He ought to be one of my *stars* – not a bit-player.

The 'gap' in such cases is between a bad or undesirable or troublesome state of affairs – *now* – and a good or desirable or more satisfying state of affairs in the *future*. In some cases, the mere *absence* of the troublesome state of affairs will do. On others a change to a new state of affairs is called for. Either way, the *problem* is that of *fixing* the status quo ... changing it into something that's either in line with expectations or simply a lot more palatable.

2. The Do-It problem

This is a bit different. Rather than being faced with a 'problem' that has to be solved, we have set or are assigned a goal or objective to be achieved. It's still a problem but it is – in most cases – a rather more *positive* problem that we have to deal with. It has the hint of a *challenge* in it.

Here are some examples of *Do-It* problems.

- The HR group has to have twenty-five new graduates hired by the end of July.
- We need to get our national account managers thinking more like true *business* people.
- We need someone to put together an employee newsletter – and you're it.
- I'd like to see more people thinking *critically* about things, questioning things, asking *why*.
- The Stoke-on-Trent plant has been given the goal of reducing inventory costs by 10 per cent.

The 'gap' in this case is really between a state of *nothingness* – the present situation isn't necessarily 'bad' – and the outcome we want to achieve. In most cases, the outcome we want to achieve is a bit on the fuzzy side and will need tightening-up. In most cases, too, there will be obstacles in the way – forces which work *against* our efforts to change things.

With a *Fix-It* problem, in other words, the focus is on the status quo side of the gap and the message is: 'Fix it'. *Make the problem go away*. With a *Do-It* problem, the focus is on the future state of affairs and the message is 'Do it'. *Move us in that direction.*

The question is – How do we get from here to there? How do we bridge the gap?

> With a Do-It problem, the focus is on the future state of affairs and the message is 'Do it'. Move us in that direction.

The problem-solving process

The problem-solving *process* is, in practice, as varied as the problems toward which it is directed.

Some problems we solve without even thinking about them. A package that was due to be mailed yesterday, and which absolutely *has* to be in the recipient's hands by tomorrow, wasn't ready for the afternoon pick-up at the post office. So we call the courier company and arrange for it to be picked up for next-day delivery. The reason we didn't have to think about it is that we've done this kind of thing before. It's the proven, tested solution that we turn to when same-day or next-day delivery is critical.

The *first* time it happened, on the other hand, necessitated some bona fide problem-solving. Do we get in the car and *drive* the package to its destination? Should we call the recipient and explain that the promised deadline isn't going to be met – that the package will arrive a day later than originally thought? Or, is there a courier service of some sort that we can turn to? If so, who? And how soon can they be here?

How much will it cost? If we call a courier company, that is. If it's going to cost an arm and a leg, then maybe we should look again at the idea of just getting in the car and *driving* the package there. Or maybe there's a bus or train service that's cheaper than courier. But could they get it there by 10.00 a.m. tomorrow? That's the rub.

Notice how one very important part of the problem-solving process is setting priorities … deciding on what can give a bit and what can't. The idea of calling the recipient and explaining that the parcel would be arriving a day late was rejected. No, it's got to be there by 10.00 a.m. tomorrow. That's a small sub-decision we made. It establishes a basic criterion that has to be satisfied and also helps move the problem-solving process forward. There's a sense, as we make that small sub-decision, that we're *getting somewhere.*

This, then, is the process of problem-solving. A package that is supposed to arrive tomorrow won't arrive on time unless we actively intervene in the situation and figure out what to do about it.

Developing a model

> You have to have a logical, step-by-step model that suits you – and you have to use it consistently.

Problem-solving is something that a lot of us take for granted. It's something we just do. But most of us haven't *trained* ourselves to be good problem-solvers or given much thought to problem-solving as a *process* subject to principles and rules and right ways of doing it and wrong ways of doing it.

The truly professional manager knows that a sound solution is the result of the systematic application of mental effort, and that the *process* of developing such a solution can be studied and learned just like any other skill.

Whether we are solving a problem ourselves or helping someone else to, the best place to begin is with a good practical understanding of the problem-solving process. A simple, easy-to-understand, step-by-step model of the problem-solving process.

> A problem is a gap between the ideal or the goal and the actual state of affairs. You begin by gathering data and defining the problem clearly. Then and only then do you start looking at solution options. You survey a full range of options, using a bit of creative brainstorming if need be, before trying to zero in on a single option ...

This is the sort of basic stuff that a model has to contain. It has to be simple, with no more than five or six steps. It has to be couched in very plain and practical terms. And, once you have it, you stick with it until it becomes a natural part of the way you look at things.

There are a lot of different models of the problem-solving process. They all represent the logical sequence of questions we should ask in answering the big question – What am I going to do?

Most authors opt for some sort of practical adaptation of the scientific method, the method which scientists use to investigate phenomena and discover principles. The critical thing isn't that you have the right model. There is no such thing, one is about as good as another. The critical thing is that you have a model in your mind and that you stick with it so that it becomes an ingrained, integral part of the way you look at things. You have to have a logical, step-by-step model that suits you – and you have to use it consistently. Even a simplistic model, ingrained in one's mind and used instinctively, is better than a much more elaborate or conceptually accurate model that is too complex or too obtuse for you or anybody else to understand and use.

Let's put together, then, a model of the problem-solving process. There are two important guidelines that we should probably keep in mind as we proceed. First, keep it simple. Second, keep it natural.

Keeping things as simple as possible

The number *seven* is important. Seven, plus or minus two, is reportedly the number of things that a human being can keep in their head – actively – at any one time. So it's a good idea to never sketch out a list or a flowchart or a diagram, if it's something you have to remember or learn to use *intuitively*, with more than seven steps in it.

And our problem-solving model is something that we want to remember and learn to use intuitively. We want it to become second-nature.

Keeping things as 'natural' as possible

We don't want to stray too far from the way you think about and solve problems right now. You might, for example, view the problem-solving process as consisting of two simple steps:

♦ I think about the problem, and then …
♦ I decide what to do.

This might raise some questions. For example, what caused you to think about the problem in the first place? Did someone bring it to your attention? Was it dumped in your lap? Is it just something that happened?

Another question might be raised about the deciding-what-to-do part of your model. *Doing things* isn't all that simple. It may require getting the time and commitment of other people, people with pressures and problems and priorities of their own. It may involve a complex sequence of action steps with lots of room for things to go askew at each step along the way. It may involve spending money, or changing the way people do things, or getting the powers that be to re-think a long-standing corporate policy.

So our two-step model might better reflect the reality of things by being expanded a bit:

- A problem comes to my attention.
- I think about the problem, and then …
- I decide what to do.
- Then I do it.

It shouldn't take too much convincing to add on a couple more steps:

- A problem comes to my attention.
- I investigate, ask a few questions, get the facts.
- I think about the problem, and then …
- I decide what to do.
- Then I do it.
- Then I look at the results to see if the problem has been solved.

The last step – looking at the results – is a useful one because it's the step that feeds back into the beginning of the process. As you look at the results of your problem-solving action, you go back to the beginning of the cycle if the problem still hasn't gone away.

A six-step model

Let's go with the six-step model depicted in Figure 7. We've broken the thinking-about-the-problem step into *two* steps – Step Three, where we define the problem, and Step Four, where we scan or generate some possible solutions. And we've left off the closing-of-the-loop portion. We'll treat that as a recycling of the process rather than as a separate 'step' therein.

Our model, then, contains six separate steps. The first three steps have to do with defining the problem: becoming aware of it,

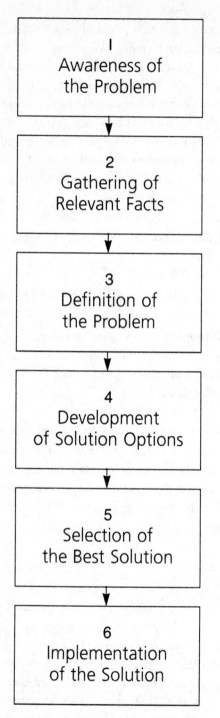

Fig. 7. Problem-solving model.

gathering information about it, and then arriving at a clear understanding of what the problem is. The next three steps move us from the understanding phase into the solution phase: exploring and developing a variety of solution options, choosing the one that promises to produce the best result, and then acting upon it.

Before discussing the various steps of the model in detail we need to clearly understand that this is just a model – not reality. In actual practice, the steps in the model do not follow one after the other in a definite and orderly fashion. There is considerable overlap amongst them, and a good deal of skipping back and forth.

So let's treat the model as a conceptual *map* rather than a literal description of what actually happens in most problem-solving situations.

And it is, as we have already agreed, an *iterative* model where Step Six connects back into Step One and re-starts the whole cycle. As we put a solution into action, we gauge its impact on the problem situation and effectively work through the six-step cycle again – until such time as we conclude that the problem has been truly 'solved' and is no longer an issue.

AIDOSE – the lunchbox edition

Figure 8 is a 'lunchbox' edition of our model. It assigns a neat one-word label to each of the six steps. Being able to assign a different letter to each of the six steps – use of the acronym A-I-D-O-S-E in other words – is also a useful way of remembering what the steps are.

Problem-solving versus decision-making

We should probably clarify these terms, and now is a good time to do so – before we get too far into our discussion.

We've said that a problem is a *gap* between the way things are and the way they ought to be. A *decision*, on the other hand, is a choice between two or more alternatives. It may involve a crisp yes-or-no answer or it may mean choosing the best from a set of alternatives which are all satisfactory. In most situations, making a decision between two or more possible solutions is a very

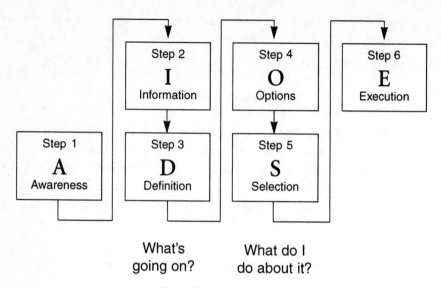

Fig. 8. The AIDOSE model.

important step in the problem-solving process. So decision-making is really a sub-set of problem-solving.

But it gets tricky. It can also be argued that decision-making, rather than being a sub-set of problem-solving, is actually a much *broader* concept. Where 'problem-solving' concerns itself with things that have already happened and is largely done by people on the lower rungs of the organisational ladder, decision-making focuses on building and shaping the future and is the province of managers at the more senior levels of the hierarchy (Figure 9).

The boundary line between problem-solving and decision-making is also made rather fuzzy by the simple fact that having to *make* a decision can be a problem. My daughter has to decide between going on a three-day trip to Ross-on-Wye with her school class, which would mean missing her weekend choir practice (with an important concert looming on the horizon), or going to the choir practice but foregoing the school trip.

That sounds like a pure 'decision' between two options. But it's also a problem that has to be solved. Having to *make* the decision in the first place – the clash between two desirable activities and hence the need to forego one in favour of the other – is the problem.

Problem-solving is:	Decision-making is:
◆ focused on the past	◆ focused on the future
◆ usually analytical	◆ often creative
◆ operational	◆ directional
◆ done at lower levels	◆ done at senior levels

Fig. 9. Problem-solving versus decision-making.

A few more examples:

- It comes down to Mike Fletcher and Ruth Shearsby. Both excellent candidates. Who gets the job?
- Jennifer has her heart set on going to Henley High, but I think she'd do better at St Joseph's.
- The fact that the product did well in the States doesn't mean that it will sell in the UK. Do we go with it?
- Do we start at the top and work down, or is this one of those situations where we use the end-run strategy?

We'll largely ignore this category of problem from here on in, mainly because it quite clearly crosses the fuzzy border that separates problem-solving from decision-making. Let's just recognise that when we give someone a tough decision to make, what we're effectively saying is – *It's your problem, you deal with it.*

Muddling through

Question – *Does the model that we are developing in this chapter reflect how managers actually solve problems … or how they could if they put their minds to it?* If it does, then that's fine. If it doesn't, then when we try to put the model into practice, we're quite likely to be disappointed with the results that we get.

Most managers would probably lay out a four- or five- or six-step model not unlike the one we are developing here. The exact definition of steps, and the wording used to describe them, would vary from manager to manager, but the core process would undoubtedly be there.

It's difficult to know, however, whether that means that this is actually how managers go about solving the problems they face on a day-to-day basis. It might be that this is simply the way they feel they *ought* to go about it. Indeed, there is some hard evidence that such is the case.

One damned thing after another

> The work of the executive is characterised by variety, fragmentation, and brevity. Managers emerge as being action-driven, short term and concrete in their thinking.

In a pioneering study back in the 1960's, Dr Rosemary Stewart asked a group of managers in the UK to track their usage of time – in great detail – over a four-week period. What emerged was a picture of the manager on the move, making decisions on the fly and stopping to interject a brief question here and there. One of Dr Stewart's findings was that the average manager, during the average month, had only *nine periods of a half-hour duration* where they were not interrupted. 'It's one damned thing after another', managers complained. 'There's no time to think'.

A few years later, Henry Mintzberg conducted a similar study – and drew similar conclusions. His main conclusion was that the work of the executive is characterised by variety, fragmentation, and brevity. They perform a great variety of tasks at a high pace and with little time to spare. Whether by choice or necessity, managers emerge from the Mintzberg study as being action-driven, short-term and concrete in their thinking, making decisions and solving problems on the fly, relying more on networking and face-to-face discussion than on reading or reflective thinking. Certainly not lining up for courses on Rational Decision-Making.

Case study: Daniel Isenberg

Perhaps our best view of the manager as a thinker is that provided by Daniel Isenberg's intense study of a dozen senior American managers and reported in his classic *Harvard Business Review* article of 1984.

*'They seldom think in ways that one might simplistically view as "rational".
They rarely systematically formulate goals, assess their worth, evaluate the
probabilities of alternative ways of reaching them, and choose the path that
maximises expected return. Rather, managers frequently bypass rigorous
analytical planning altogether – particularly when they face difficult, novel, or
extremely entangled problems. When they do use analysis for a prolonged
time, it is always in conjunction with intuition.'*

To the extent that managers use a step-by-step problem-solving process at all,
Isenberg noted, they often appear to skip back and forth amongst the steps
rather than going through them in sequence.

*'The two stages of problem analysis and problem solving are tightly linked
and occur reiteratively rather than sequentially. By going back and forth
between these two cognitive processes, managers define the array of
problems facing them in terms that already incorporate key features of
solutions and that thus make it easier for them to take action.'* _____

The implications

Let's go back to our question. Does our step-by-step problem-
solving model stand up in practice?

By and large, it doesn't. Managers don't make much use of a
formal, step-by-step model of the problem-solving process
although the people who write their briefing papers, or who stand
up in meetings and present well-researched options for
discussion, might well do.

There in the background

> Have a model of the problem-solving process. It's there in the
> background guiding our thinking.

Let's not throw the baby out with the bathwater. Just because what
we see on the surface bears little relation to our formal, step-by-
step model there is no reason to declare the model out of touch
with reality and throw it out entirely.

Having a model of the problem-solving process gives us a goal
to aim for. It serves as a useful warning to go one step at a time. It

also gives us a frame of reference, a common language, in our discussions with colleagues and subordinates.

And, most importantly, it's there in the background, guiding our thinking, even when we are not conscious of its playing an active role.

The challenge

The challenge we face, in becoming more effective as problem-solvers and decision-makers, is that of *starting* with a stepwise model and using it effectively *regardless*. Using it effectively in the sense of adapting it to the realities of the environment and knowing precisely where, when, how and why it has to be adapted as we use it in practise.

And those are just some of the things we are going to look at in the chapters ahead. The need for judgement. The human factor. The need to 'sell' one's solutions. Techniques for thinking along more creative lines.

Summary

In Chapter 2 we covered the importance of thinking straight and were introduced to a problem-solving model:

+ A *problem* is a gap between the way things are and the way they ought to be. Problem-solving is the process we use to close the gap.
+ Problem-solving is something that a lot of us take for granted. Like public speaking or chairing meetings, it's something we just *do*.
+ The truly professional manager, however, knows that problem-solving can be studied and learned just like any other skill.
+ The best place to begin is with a step-by-step model of the problem-solving process – the simpler and more natural the model, the better.
+ The key thing is to find or develop a model and stick with it so that it becomes a natural, integral part of the way we look at things.
+ Our AIDOSE model contains six separate steps – six main sub-processes which find their way into most problem-solving situations.

- In actual practice, there is considerable overlap amongst the model's six steps, and a good deal of skipping back and forth between them.
- The model is an *iterative* one. What that means is that Step Six connects back into Step One and re-starts the whole cycle.
- Studies have shown that, in reality, managers don't solve problems in the orderly, 'rational' way suggested by a six-step model.
- Still, having a model of the problem-solving process is useful. It guides our thinking, even if we are not conscious of it doing so.
- Our challenge in becoming more effective problem-solvers is to recognise the model's limitations and use it effectively *regardless*.

CHAPTER 3

Becoming Aware of the Problem

T he first step in the problem-solving process is to become aware of the problem – to recognise that something isn't the way it should be.

Something comes to our attention. Things aren't happening quite the way we want them to happen. A project is falling further and further behind schedule.

All these are signals that a problem exists. All we want to do at this point is state it in words.

- Sales to drugstore chains are off by 20 per cent.
- Administration costs are way out of line.
- Jim's proposal can't go out the way it is.
- My husband has hardly said a word all evening.
- I just can't see where the school fees will come from.

And then – we ask ourselves four simple questions.

Four simple questions

What we do when a problem first presents itself is crucial. And the best way to react is to close the door, clear the desk, take a deep breath, and calmly run through the following four questions.

1. What – exactly – is the problem?

Okay, we've just lost the Hollander account. There's a good degree of urgency associated with it, because it's an important account.

The first thing we have to do is ascertain exactly what has happened. Who called whom? What was said? When Frank says that we've 'lost' the Hollander account, what exactly is he implying? It could be any one of a *number* of things …

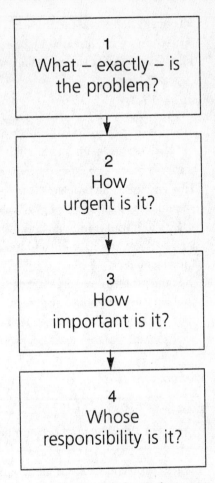

Fig. 10. Four simple questions.

- Laura Riggins, their buyer, is hopping mad and is threatening to cancel their business with us.
- Laura said something that seemed to *imply* that she was going to cancel their business with us.
- She has just signed a two-year contract with one of our chief competitors, effectively shutting us out.
- Frances Muirhead, Laura's boss and the category manager, has opted to go with the competition.
- Frank has really screwed something up badly and is *afraid* that we might end up losing the Hollander business.

None of these five things constitute *good* news, but they are not all equally bad – and they have different connotations in regard to the action we might wish to take at this stage. So it is important to know exactly what we are dealing with.

2. How urgent is it?

> If crisis management is the order of the day in your job, then *that* in itself is a problem that has to be addressed.

How urgent is the problem? Is the problem urgent enough that I should clear the decks and give it absolute top priority?

Or can it wait until tomorrow? Should we slide it in as a high-priority item and have Bill and Judy get to work on it first thing in the morning?

Some problems *are* urgent. Let's acknowledge that. But such problems are very much the exception rather than the rule. Or they ought to be. If crisis management is the order of the day in your job, then *that* in itself is a problem that has to be addressed.

3. How important is it?

> We can't afford to allow *urgency* alone to govern our response to problems. The *importance* factor has to enter as well.

Urgent problems clamour for attention. They press themselves upon us and demand a response. But that doesn't necessarily reflect their *importance* in the overall scheme of things. Fixing a flat tyre on your car is urgent. You can't drive unless you do it. But so is getting your oil changed regularly if you want a car you can rely on.

We can't afford to allow *urgency* alone to govern our response to problems. The *importance* factor has to be entered into the equation as well. Take, as an example, what we just said about crisis management … if it is a daily feature of the work you do, then *that* in itself is a problem that you ought to be addressing.

That's a logical statement, and a good idea. But when and how would we actually address the problem? Would it mean closing the office door and asking our PA to hold all our calls while we think about the issue? Or would we think about it in the car on the way home?

And then, of course, the real question. Assuming that we say yes to either of these options, *will we actually do it?*

4. *Whose responsibility is it?*

Whose problem is it? No – that's not the right way to phrase things. It's *our* problem. Whose *responsibility* is it? That's better. Whose job is it to carry the ball, to spearhead our response, to take the lead?

> The important thing is that the problem be addressed by the right people at the right time – and that you be responsible for activating and managing the process.

Clearly, problem-solving is your responsibility. However, resolving to close the door and *think* about the issue is futile, because we both know that that isn't going to happen. A decision to think about the issue while you're driving along the M25 or the M1 is more likely to be acted upon, but how *effective* is your thinking likely to be while you're trying to keep an eye on the traffic at the same time?

But the more important point is that addressing the issue may not even be something that you should be doing all by yourself. It makes much more sense, in this specific case, to have a working lunch. And you might want, before you have that lunch, to consult with someone in your area to see whether they can shed some light on the situation or come up with some ideas for putting a solution in place.

The point is this. Yes, you're responsible for seeing that the problem is dealt with. But no, you don't have to deal with it yourself. Not directly. The important thing is that the problem be addressed by the right people at the right time – and that you be responsible for activating and managing the process.

Our first reaction – the pitfalls

Let's talk again about how we react to a problem when it first presents itself. There are three thoughts which are quite likely to pass through our mind:

◆ *This is a problem.*

+ *I've got to solve it.*
+ *I'd better do something.*

We can't take these assumptions at face value, and we certainly shouldn't *act* upon them. If we do, then we fall into one of the four major pitfalls which await the unwary in the first stage of the problem-solving process.

> We can't – we shouldn't – take these assumptions at face value, and we certainly shouldn't act upon them.

1. Jumping too quickly into action

> Nine times out of ten, if we just take action or bark out an order, right then and there, we'll be wrong.

The first question we generally ask ourselves when we discover a problem is *What do we do?* There's nothing wrong with that – as long as we don't answer it right away. The fact that we ask the question is a useful reminder that we want to take action in a way that solves the problem.

When we first see a problem it may seem quite straightforward. And, in our eagerness to come to grips with the situation it is very tempting to plunge ahead.

But – nine times out of ten, if we just take action or bark out an order, right then and there, we'll be wrong. At some point we'll discover that we have been nibbling away ineffectually at the fringes of the real problem or perhaps even working on the wrong problem altogether.

In all but the simplest problem situations, there is no obvious right action to take. If there was, the situation would hardly warrant being called a problem, and it certainly shouldn't have been brought to our attention. Someone else should have handled it. Routinely.

2. Treating symptoms rather than causes

> The best way is to proceed the way a good physician proceeds when a patient complains about a headache or blurriness of vision. He treats them as symptoms.

Far more often than they should, managers make decisions without having clearly defined the problem they are trying to solve. In other words, they skip Step Two – the gathering of relevant facts – and Step Three – the definition of the problem.

The best way is to proceed the way a good physician proceeds when a patient complains about a headache or blurriness of vision or lack of appetite. A good physician treats these as symptoms and then proceeds to question, probe and experiment until they can say with a high degree of certainty that the problem has been pinned down. Once that has been done, the solution is usually obvious.

Assume that what you're seeing is merely a signal. A symptom. As such, it's important but its importance lies strictly in the fact that it has drawn our attention. We recognise that a problem exists.

3. *Assuming that you have to solve it*

> Your role as manager is more that of a problem *discoverer* than a problem *solver*.

The rule of thumb here is *don't*. Don't assume that the problem is yours to solve. More often than not, it won't be.

If you are a manager your role is more that of a problem *discoverer* than a problem *solver*. That's where you add your value and make your vital contribution. And there are a number of ways in which the value you add is unique. You are in a position to take the overview on a key issue – to see the Big Picture, to relate the specifics of this one situation to the more general issues at stake.

Even if you're *not* a manager – in the formal sense that there are no people reporting to you and to whom you can freely delegate things – that still doesn't mean that you have to solve every problem that you come across.

It means thinking not just like a manager, but like a chief executive officer or managing director. And what the latter does is ask a simple question: *Who's the single person in this organisation best equipped or best positioned to solve this problem?* Is this a problem that I should be dealing with? Would I be better to spend a half-hour briefing Harriet and turning the whole situation over to her?

As a rule, most of us – unless we're senior managers – are reluctant to assign problems to people over whom we have no authority. Who are *we*, after all, to tell Harriet that we've decided that she is the single person in this organisation best equipped or best positioned to solve this problem?

One of our *Famous Five* – Graeme Weir, manufacturing director for a Leamington-based producer of automotive components – answered the question this way:

> '*I want my people to be thinking like mini-CEO's. It really bothers me when I see someone wasting a whole afternoon struggling with a problem that they are not equipped to handle. Why not make an executive decision – show some initiative – and pass the problem along to the right person? That's what I want my people to be doing. Thinking, and acting, like executives rather than junior supervisors.*'

Why not? It makes sense. But, for the average corporation, such a simple idea represents an enormous turnaround in the way we think about things. What would it be like to work in a hassle-free, problem-free environment – where everyone is well-motivated and competent and superbly trained, where your customers are happy and your shareholders are content and your share of the market is downright sinful …?

Worrisome.

Life shouldn't be like that. And on those rare days when it seems that way, you should very quickly set about creating a disturbance of some sort. To create the demand for something a bit more innovative and a bit more daring than what we did yesterday.

> One of a manager's most crucial roles is that of *tension-creator*. You should set about creating a disturbance.

The point we're making, of course, is that one of a manager's most crucial roles is that of *tension-creator*. No one has said it better than Murray Lincoln, the well-known American co-operative leader.

'Any organisation, once it becomes successful, is apt to lose its original drive and vision. Because this is so, I've often suggested that we have a vice-president in charge of revolution. He'd be one man not responsible for any operations. He'd stand to one side, with whatever staff he needed, to pick holes in whatever we were doing and remind us of our basic philosophy, our fundamental concepts. His job would be to stir up everything and everybody, to criticise and challenge everything being done – objectives, methods, programmes, results. Executives get into ruts … I would want my vice-president in charge of revolution to spend time throwing us off balance, shaking us out of our coziness, making us feel a little insecure and uncertain.'

The 'Oh-Sh-t' Problem

We have been implying all along that some problems are *urgent* and have to be dealt with as such.

- I'm going to be late for the meeting.
- I'm going to have to skip the meeting altogether.
- The report didn't go out as promised.
- They didn't get the report.
- Bill Harris won't be coming.
- Has anyone seen Barbara?
- We're out of Number 17 washers.

We've used the term 'crisis management'. The *'Oh Sh-t'* label is an alternate term which captures how problems of this ilk are described by practising managers.

Such problems, we agreed, should be the exception rather than the rule. Be that as it may, let's talk briefly about how to deal with them.

First of all, accept what has happened. Calmly and objectively. Don't fret about what you can't change. The deadline is here and the report isn't done. The funding you were counting on has been reduced by half. Focus all your attention on what has to happen *now* – and an hour from now, and tomorrow, and the day after – in order to make the best of a bad situation.

The only time you look backwards is when you need information. What, for example, do we mean when we say that the project has been sidetracked? Sidetracked in what sense? Where *exactly* do things stand? Let's be precise about it so that we know what we're dealing with.

And then – *visualise the end result.* Visualise a successful conclusion to the whole sordid affair. Okay, the people on the receiving end, be it a customer or otherwise, aren't happy with what happened but at least they feel that you handled it professionally and salvaged what you could for them. If anything, you've won points for your diligence in responding promptly, professionally and maybe even creatively to an unfortunate turn of events.

And then, figure out how you achieved that positive outcome. Work backwards. What exactly did you do that led to the reasonably palatable state of affairs which we have just described? Who did you call or talk to? What did you say? What actions were taken, and who exactly was involved in taking them?

Finally, make it happen. Get started. The sooner the better.

Keeping your antenna up

One of our biggest challenges as managers is to avoid getting so *tied up* with specific meetings and activities that we stop having time for just getting out there and sniffing around to see what's happening.

To close out this chapter, let's look briefly at some ways of heightening our awareness of problems and potential problems.

Get out there and walk around

Good managers 'manage' by walking around.

You're not going to become aware of problems if you're sitting behind your desk, diligently reading your way through a thirty-page report. You might become aware of certain specific problems described in the report but things that are written up in a report are rarely urgent. By and large, if they have to do with problems at all, they have to do with problems which have already been acted upon or at least identified and allocated to someone for handling.

No, to become *aware* of problems you have to be out there where things are happening, not stuck in your office. Good managers make it a practise to do a lot of what most of us have learned to call 'managing by walking around'. They recognise the importance of getting out there and they make time for it.

Take samples

When, in your travels, you pop your head into Jim Pascoe's office and ask him how the revision of the divisional marketing plan is coming along, he's probably going to tell you that it's coming along quite well, thank you very much. He's unlikely to give you much more than the most general of overviews because he doesn't want to take up too much of your time or bore you with a lot of details.

Still, it wouldn't hurt to probe for some specific details on one or two key points. High-level executives often do this as a way of *sampling* the person's thinking. If the person can give you a lucid, coherent response to just one or two probing questions, then you can walk away with the assurance that they probably have things well under control.

Stay close to the customer

It is especially important that you stay close to the customer.

The reason is simple. It is better to become aware of a problem by hearing through the grapevine that your customer has been talking to the competition than by seeing – two months later – a sudden drop in the amount of product being sold into that account. In the first instance, you have time to do something proactive to maintain your edge. In the second, it's too late.

It is better to have the head of a department express, over sandwiches and coffee in the cafeteria, a mild concern about what they feel is an insufficient sense of *urgency* on the part of one of your people than to have things get so bad that your common superior has to step in and sort out a very messy situation.

The lunch in the cafeteria with your opposite number, your attendance at the monthly trade meeting, or the annual conference, your half-hour chat on the telephone with one of your major customers are all wise investments of your time. They allow you to keep in touch with what's happening, and to spot issues before they blossom into full-blown problems. If a problem *does* occur, they allow you to understand much more quickly and astutely why it has occurred and what has to be done about it.

Trust your instincts

Problems sometimes come to our attention in very tenuous, hazy, ill-defined forms.

For some people, this lack of precision doesn't present a problem. They take pride in having a good 'feel' for things and have learned to trust it when it's time to make a decision.

For other people, however, the idea of moving ahead on the basis of something as nebulous as one's *instinct* would be uncomfortable if not totally unthinkable.

And it's not just accountants and engineers who think that way. It has long been recognised that the way people think tends to lean distinctly toward one of two poles. There's a linear, sequential, logical, analytical mode of thinking that is supposedly related to the left hemisphere of the human brain and is hence called left-brain thinking. And there is a holistic, relational, non-linear way of thinking which is associated with the brain's *right* hemisphere and is therefore referred to as right-brain thinking. Although it's difficult to be terribly exact about these things, if you stopped a hundred commuters at Charing Cross station and gave them each a brief test of left-versus-right-brain dominance, you would probably find that you had about an equal number of each.

If you're a *left-brain* sort of person, you'll have to make a special effort to learn to trust your instincts. A good manager can *sense* that something is awry long before the average manager *reads* about it in the form of a worrisome dip in a vital statistic or ratio.

Whether we can actually *develop* our instincts, in the sense of making them *stronger* or more *acute*, is debatable. What we can do is recognise their importance as a monitoring device and pay attention when they make their presence felt.

Look in the mirror

> The problem that we are *least* likely to be aware of is the one that stems from the way we do things …

The problem that we are *least* likely to be aware of is the one that involves *us* – as a manager. The one that stems from the way we do things:

- We're overbearing.
- We put people off.
- We're too quick to jump in and do people's thinking for them.
- We get impatient with people.
- We seem reluctant to come right out and tell people what to do.
- We spend too much time behind closed doors.

Coming to terms with the truth about ourselves is difficult. Think, for example, of how it feels when you hear your voice on a tape recording or video. Is my voice really that tinny? Do I really start so many sentences without finishing them? Do I really sound that nervous and insecure about myself?

If you are in a position to influence how your company trains its managers, push for the use of real, live feedback on real, live behaviour. That's how people learn best. At some point, you have to be given a chance to try it out and then be given helpful feedback on how you are doing.

The suggestion here is that you create such learning experiences for yourself. Jack Carter, one of our *Famous Five*, put it this way:

> *'I've been in discussion groups – they used to call them T-Groups – where people are supposed to "open up" with one another, usually with the help of a moderator and some special exercises. The idea's okay, but the whole thing left a sour taste in people's mouths. A couple of years ago, I started using 360° feedback, just within my own team of people. What it does is give me some hard data on how I actually behave as a manager, and what impact that has on people. And that, believe me, is powerful.'*

When and wherever possible – routinise

You may recall that in the last chapter, we talked about a package that was due to be mailed, which *had* to be in the recipient's hands by tomorrow, and which wasn't ready for the afternoon post. The *first* time it happened, we had a bona fide problem-solving situation on our hands. The *second* and *third* time it happened, on the other hand, we knew what to do. We didn't have to think about it.

> Every time we routinise something, it's one less problem to solve. One less decision to make. One less thing to think about.

The idea here is to *routinise* problems wherever we can and to conserve our problem-solving energy and creativity for those situations which are truly new and different. Routinising may be as simple as making a mental note of what we did. Or it might mean writing up a procedure and pasting it into the operations manual. Somewhere between these two extremes, we might find ourselves letting people know through simple word-of-mouth that such-and-such a problem ought to be dealt with in such-and-such a way.

The benefits of doing so should be obvious. Every time we routinise something it's one less problem to solve.

Put controls in place

This is one specific way of routinising a problem – putting some sort of control in place so that you know when something needs to be attended to *before it* becomes a problem. If our profit projections for the month of April are out of line because of an unexpected increase in administrative costs then let's put something in place that warns us in advance when this is going to happen.

If we can't get an important document off the fax machine because the machine is out of paper and there's no more in the storage cupboard, then let's have someone keep track of our office supplies inventory so that it doesn't happen again.

And finally ...

If you don't have a problem, find one!

If it ain't broke, break it! The idea is basically the same. If good results are being pumped out of the system a bit too smoothly and effortlessly, then what you might want to do is to assume that disaster lies just around the corner. The competition is just about to come out with something that even your most loyal customers will find irresistible. Three of your best performers will march into your office the day after tomorrow and announce that they have decided to go into business for themselves and will be leaving at the end of the month.

So this is no time to be complacent. What can we do, starting today, to cement our relationships with customers, to add extra value to what we do, to make the best products on the market even better?

In other words, if you don't have a problem to solve, *create* one.

Summary

In Chapter 3 we have looked at the importance of starting the problem-solving cycle in an organised manner.

- Avoid jumping in with both feet every time something untoward happens. Not every symptom heralds a problem requiring active attention.
- Treat red flags as symptoms rather than causes until further investigation has been done. Proceed the way a good physician would.
- Treat a crisis like a crisis. Move quickly, confidently, and authoritatively in those situations where decisive action is required.
- If crisis management has become a dominant feature of your job, then *that* in itself is a problem that has to be addressed.
- Focus on *delegating* rather than *doing* where someone else is better equipped or positioned to deal with the problem.
- Having 'problems' isn't necessarily bad or undesirable. Indeed, one of a manager's most crucial roles is that of a *tension-creator*.
- One of our biggest challenges as managers is to keep time available for just getting out there to see what's happening.
- Our initial awareness of a problem is often *instinctive* – and we have to learn to trust our instincts and value them as an early warning system.
- Every time we *routinise* something, it's one less problem to solve.
- Cultivate specific people best positioned to alert you to potential problems before they become problems.

CHAPTER 4

Gathering the Relevant Facts

B efore we decide what to do, before we even say that we know for sure what the real problem is ... we have to go through the discipline of gathering the facts.

And it *does* involve discipline. It is so tempting to skimp a bit at this stage in the problem-solving cycle. To get on with the much more 'managerial' tasks of coming out with a crisp and confident statement of what the problem is. But *gathering facts*? That almost sounds as if we're taking refuge in *inaction*. Not *doing* anything about the problem.

We know, of course, that such is not the case. And we will re-confirm it in this chapter. But 'fact-finding' *does* have a rather mundane, non-managerial ring to it and there is a natural tendency to work our way through this step rather quickly and superficially if not skip it altogether.

Getting good information

To understand the problem, to understand the real problem, we need to collect and analyse the *critical* facts relevant to the situation. Indeed, we have to go further than that. We have to understand what they mean.

We have to be focused

It is important that we never forget *why* we are searching for information, and what that information has to do for us.

- ◆ In the case of a *Fix-It* problem, our goal is to find out what is *causing* the problem.
- ◆ In the case of a *Do-It* problem, our goal is to clarify where we want to end up and where we are starting from.

We have to keep our goal clearly in mind. We don't stop gathering information until the goal has been achieved. But, when it has been achieved, we stop.

> It is important that we never forget *why* we are searching for information, and what that information has to do for us.

We have to be selective

Fact-finding has to be a sharply focused effort. We need to decide what information is going to be essential and what is not. Otherwise, we may end up moving ahead on the basis of a large array of facts and yet have relatively little information on the most significant aspects of the problem. So we have to be selective.

More than anything else, what should be guiding our information-gathering activity is a knowledge of how we will want to define the problem. In our case, as we saw in the last chapter, defining the problem will involve filling in four boxes – *Symptoms, Causes, Outcomes,* and *Constraints.*

It also lends a clear sense of *purpose* to our information gathering. We gather information about the problem so that we can arrive at an *understanding* of the problem, and the reason we want to understand the problem is so that we can decide what to *do* about it. Each step is a link in the chain.

Case study: Jennifer Adair _____

Jennifer Adair, Customer Service Manager with a London-based tour operator and one of our *Famous Five*, described the reality of how this is done:

'I sniff around for information, usually by talking informally with people – in their office, over lunch, before or after a meeting – and then perhaps raising the issue briefly during a team meeting. At this stage, I don't need all the details. What I want to understand is how people are being affected. How is the problem interfering with their getting things done? Is there an impact on the delivery of service? At a later stage, once we've put a task force together or I've given someone the job of taking things further, we can worry about the details. It's the overview that I'm after. The outcomes.' _____

We have to look for meaning

We have to figure out what the facts mean. We have to recognise that facts invariably deal with past history, and we're using them to help guide future action. So we have to draw intelligent inferences. The facts alone have little or nothing to tell us.

Back to Jennifer:

> *'Is this a one-off problem or a systems problem? That's one of the first questions I ask myself. If it's a one-off problem, and the person involved hasn't been able to solve it, then often all I have to do is give him or her a little nudge in the right direction or nod my approval for something they want to do. But if it's what I call a 'systems' problem – something that has to do with how we deal with a whole class of customer-related problems, let's say – then I'll get a lot more involved because we're looking at something which will probably have a bearing on how the team as a whole operates.'*

Asking the right questions

> Fact-finding, as part of the problem-solving cycle, is largely a matter of asking ourselves the right questions.

Fact-finding is largely a matter of asking ourselves the right questions. For example:

- *What* has happened, and precisely *how* did it happen? What we want to do here is turn to firsthand information. We want to make sure that we examine the situation from every viewpoint and arrive at an assessment that everyone involved concurs with.
- *Where* and *when* did the problem occur? Is the location or the time factor of significance? Why has the trouble emerged primarily in the assembly area? And why *now*?
- *Who* are the people involved in the situation, and in what way does their, or did their, involvement affect the situation? Will they continue to be involved in the future? Can we expect their behaviour to change in any way?
- *Why* hasn't the situation resolved itself? It doesn't seem that complicated. Surely someone should have looked into it by now and sorted things out.

Notice the magic words. *What, where, when, who, why.* These are good words to be using, because they're *inquisitive* words.

They're the words of someone who's looking for an answer and hasn't found it yet.

They don't have to be asked in precisely this form. And there will undoubtedly be some very specific questions that we can add in any given situation ...

- Are other companies having the same problem?
- Has Linda been told about this?
- At exactly what time did the telephone call come through?
- Is it the same machine that we had trouble with last week?
- Has anyone seen Sean?

In practice, then, what we use to gather information is a combination of the open-ended *what-where-when-who-why* queries and situation-specific questions of a more closed or pointed form. One question should lead to another. That's something you should be keenly aware of as you work through the problem. It's a sign that you're *digging*, that your questions – or, more precisely, the *answers* you get – are *leading* you somewhere.

Getting out and talking to people

> It is generally good to solicit some individual opinions and observations before going after the same information using a *group* format.

The above section underscores the importance of asking questions. In most situations, the best way to gather information about a problem is to get out there and talk to the people involved:

- So what's happening, Jim?
- When did you first notice something was wrong?
- Any idea which direction it came from?
- What do you think would happen if we removed it?
- Has all this had any effect on the work you do?
- How do things look from where you sit, Karen?
- Any idea what we should be doing about all this?
- Anything I've missed?

What we're doing here is collecting individual opinions and viewpoints. That means we should decide in advance who to talk to and what specific ground to cover with our queries.

We'll keep the questions nice and relaxed and informal but that doesn't imply that we can go round and waste either our time or theirs.

It is generally good to solicit some individual opinions and observations using a *group* format. Once people gather together around a conference table, there are usually two or three members of the team who become less forthcoming than they would be in a one-on-one situation.

Thinking = asking questions

Thinking means asking yourself questions, and then working hard to answer those questions.

Tough questions. Questions that require hard thinking and a refusal to stop until you feel that a tough question has been answered.

- Why isn't the problem showing up in the other departments?
- Why now – rather than, let's say, a month ago?
- How are the members of the board likely to react?
- What is this problem *costing* us?
- What would happen if we left the problem alone?

Tapping other sources

What we do after talking to people will depend on the sort of information we need to gather and the sort of problem we are dealing with.

If sales of one of our products has been sluggish, we'll need some data to tell us just how badly things have fallen off and where exactly that has happened. That sort of information should be on the computer somewhere. If it can't be printed out at the press of a key or two, find someone who knows about computers and have him or her figure out how to extract precisely the information you need in the form that you need it.

If the problem is a suspected failure of our product on the floor of a customer's manufacturing facility, we'll want someone out on the floor as quickly as possible to find out how *our* product is performing and to solve the customer's problem whatever the cause.

If the problem has to do with competitive activity, or trends in the industry at large, then we'll want to talk to people in our own company who are well-positioned to talk about what is happening out there. Jim, for example, who just joined us from a senior position with one of our chief competitors. Or Jane, who has just returned from a conference in Atlanta.

Let's note, incidentally, that we are talking primarily about *Fix-It* problems at this stage – problems involving a variance or an obstacle or a crisis of some sort. *Do-It* problems, where the challenge is to find a way to move toward a positive objective, also involve the gathering of information but of a slightly different sort. We'll come back to this point shortly.

Representing the facts

> Our aim should be to get the facts on paper *succinctly*, where we can see them *at a glance*.

The idea of 'representing' refers to capturing the facts in statistical form, building them into a diagram or even just *writing them down*. Getting them on paper *succinctly*, in fact, where we can hopefully see them *at a glance*. This is especially important when it is difficult to hold all the information about the problem in our mind at one time and think about it coherently. And yet it is in regard to just this sort of problem that we need to be able to stand back and look at things holistically to see what is going on.

Getting the facts down on paper has one additional benefit. It means that we don't have to carry them around in our head. And that means that we have more of our grey cells available for *thinking* about the problem. Your mind should be reserved for thinking, not used as a storage house.

Doing a force-field analysis

The idea of doing a force-field analysis is a simple but very useful way of looking at the dynamics of a problem situation.

It shows, in graphic form, the forces working for and against a particular state of affairs. It is assumed that, in a given situation, the status quo is an *equilibrium* which is being maintained by a combination of forces – some pushing the equilibrium toward a

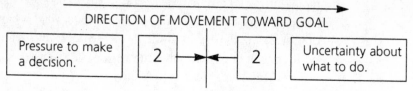

Fig. 11. Force field analysis.

goal or objective and others, the restraining or opposing forces, resisting that push.

Figure 11 illustrates the basics. We have to make a decision. We're running low on A773 blue ink, and the paint shop is asking whether it should use up what's left or rework its schedule so that the A773 blue won't be needed until tomorrow morning. There are several other complications. The likelihood of incurring overtime, the need for shipping to adjust its plans, and so on.

There are two forces acting on the situation, shown in Figure 11 – the pressure to decide and the uncertainty about what to do. The pressure and the uncertainty are acting in equal – let's make them both 2 on a scale from 1 (mild) to 3 (high) – but opposite directions to bring the whole problem-solving process to a halt.

To *change* things, to allow the equilibrium to move toward the objective of resolving the situation through making a decision, we have two choices. First, we can up the pressure. *For God's sake, we have to make a decision!*

Second, we can *reduce* the force on the right, the uncertainty about what to do. We can do that by following a rule. Then we'll write it into the operations manual so that similar situations can be handled quite routinely in future. The rule might be something like this:

♦ If re-scheduling means that shipping has to break up a full truck load, don't do it. Otherwise, re-schedule. Or ...

♦ Speak to Sam. Sam's been here seventeen years and he knows all about these things. Or ...

♦ Ask the paint shop supervisor what he thinks ought to be done and then tell him to go ahead and do it.

The beauty of a force-field analysis is that it forces us to recognise that the way things are is the result of forces acting to produce a temporary equilibrium – and that *reducing* the forces working *against* us is just as valid as increasing the forces that are moving us toward the goal.

> *Reducing* the forces working *against* what we want to achieve is just as valid a strategy as increasing the forces that are moving us toward the goal

Case Study – quitting smoking

Let's get away from the business world for a minute and assume that our problem is that of quitting smoking.

Let's subject the problem to a force-field analysis. It means drawing a diagram (Figure 12) and entering what we know into the diagram in the form of *arrows*. On the left side we'll draw arrows representing all the things that are pushing us toward the goal of quitting smoking. All the reasons that we use to talk ourselves into quitting.

On the right side of the diagram, we draw an arrow for each of the things that is *preventing* us from quitting.

As a strategy for getting us to quit smoking, there are a *number* of things we can do. Our scepticism regarding the health risks associated with smoking could be *reduced* if our doctor announces that we're now a high-risk candidate for a stroke or

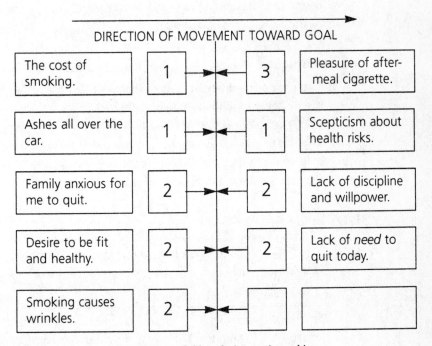

Fig. 12. Force field analysis to quit smoking.

heart attack and that, if we want to be around for Christmas, we should give up smoking *immediately*. Our rather mild concern about ashes in the car can be heightened if we suddenly find ourselves with a brand-new, sweet-smelling, smoke-free Rover in the driveway.

There are lots of ways to move the equilibrium toward the right-hand side of the diagram. And the good thing about using a force-field analysis is that it helps us identify a wider array of strategies than we might otherwise examine.

Including feelings

Feelings often need to be included in our fact-gathering. In the force-field analysis we just did for quitting-smoking we could have added one more item to our list of forces pushing us *toward* quitting. I'm *tired* of smoking. I so badly *want* to quit. I want to feel *good* about myself. I don't *want* to be a smoker any more.

That's probably the best reason of all for quitting. I just want to do it. So we enter it as an arrow in our force-field diagram. A *big* arrow, because it's an important factor. And when we do that, the whole balance of the diagram shifts. Recognising the *feeling* component has inched us ever so closer to the point where a positive decision can be made.

Other techniques

There are a few different ways to represent information and we are briefly going to look at some of them here.

The key point is that *how* you lay information out is very important. You have to choose a method that acts *effectively* to help you spot the informational gaps and develop a sense of how the data you have gathered all *adds up*.

SWOT analysis

> The SWOT model plays a helpful role by simply forcing us to put something into each of the four boxes. It forces us to be comprehensive.

Strengths, Weaknesses, Opportunities, Threats – that's what the letters SWOT stand for. The model provides four boxes into which the information we collect can be channelled (Figure 13).

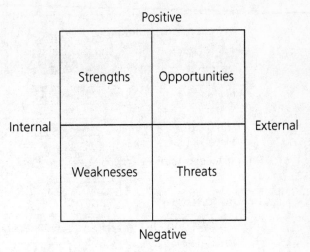

Fig. 13. SWOT analysis model.

Like any other collection of boxes, the SWOT model plays a
helpful role by simply forcing us to put something into each of
the four boxes. We know what our *strengths* are; how about our
weaknesses? The model works its magic, in other words, by simply
posing the questions.

Pareto charts

A *Pareto* chart is a vertical bar chart designed to direct our
attention away from the trivial data and toward the information
that counts. The example in Figure 14 maps out the frequency of
time-lost accidents across six different areas within a production
site, starting with the metal stamping area, where 16 of the total of
42 accidents occurred. The 16 accidents represent 38 per cent of
the total. The next area, Assembly Line A, had 11 accidents – or 26
per cent of the total. And so on.

What is interesting is the plotting of the *cumulative* percentage
of accidents using the *light* grey bar. It answers a very important
question – *Which specific areas of the plant are accounting for 80
per cent of our accidents?* Clearly, the answer is the metal stamping
area, assembly line A, and, for some reason, the paint shop. These
three areas alone account for 81 per cent of our accidents.

Knowing that, we can direct our information-gathering
activities in a much more focused manner. It allows us to use a
three-stage strategy (Figure 15) for gathering information about
the problem.

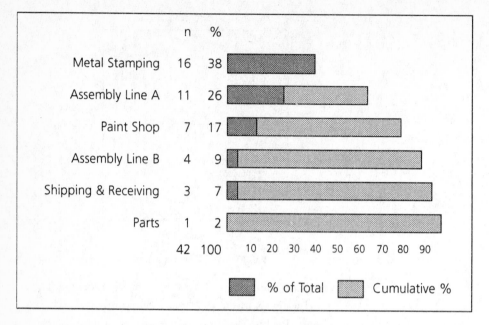

	n	%
Metal Stamping	16	38
Assembly Line A	11	26
Paint Shop	7	17
Assembly Line B	4	9
Shipping & Receiving	3	7
Parts	1	2
	42	100

% of Total   Cumulative %

Fig. 14. Pareto chart model.

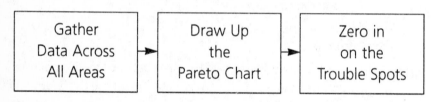

Fig. 15. Three stage strategy.

Statistical analysis

Figure 16 shows the correlations between the various dimensions on a personality profile and success in a managerial role. The profile was used to give us a rough picture of the 'personality' which managers were bringing with them into the managerial role, and 'success' was measured using overall performance ratings supplied by the managers' respective superiors.

If our 'problem' is to help our middle management team make the transition from a control-oriented way of managing to a newer, more consultative style of management – and if *one* part of our strategy for doing so is to make sure that the right people get promoted in the first place rather than going by seniority alone – then the data in Figure 16 is clearly going to be relevant. It helps

	Dimension	*r*
1	Cognitive Complexity	.47
2	Action Orientation	.42
3	Willingness to Bend	.39
4	Innovativeness	.36
5	Tough-Mindedness	.34

Fig. 16. Correlations between personality dimensions and managerial performance.

us understand what sort of people are achieving the best results as managers. It gives us *hard* data that we can use to guide our selection and development efforts.

This is *statistical* information. The common thread is that raw information is *treated* using some sort of statistical transformation, and that the latter allows certain trends or conclusions to stand out clearly in a way that would otherwise be impossible.

Behavioural observation

Actually *watching* people perform their jobs is becoming an increasingly important means of gathering data.

There is no substitute for first-hand observation of a good performer at work. It is the single best way to gain insight into the reality of a job, and into the myriad of specific things that a top performer does that sets them apart from the average performer.

And then – an interview with the person whose performance we have been observing.

The key in the interview is to dig for behavioural specifics and link these to the outcomes produced. If someone tells us they *listen well*, we have to come right back and ask what is meant by that. *You listen well in what sense? What do you actually do? What's different about the way you listen?* And then we have to find out how this produces outcomes. *And how does that make you successful? What does it actually allow you to do or achieve?*

We might find, for example, that the person listens *actively*. They nod their head from time to time, thoughtfully, in a way that shows that they are not only listening but also *thinking* about what is being said. The person chuckles, or grunts, or smiles, or looks quizzical ... not only listening but *reacting* and *appreciating*. And, periodically, they probe for a bit more detail, asking the customer to clarify or to expand upon a point.

And how does all this produce outcomes? It builds rapport, and rapport builds relationships. It encourages the customer to talk, and it is only then that we can find out what the customer needs, where things stand, what concerns they have. Our active probing also acts to *move the customer's thinking ahead.*

A blank pad of paper

In many ways, the best tool for laying out information is a blank pad of A4 or A3 paper along with a supply of pens and coloured markers.

There's a certain art to note-taking. Research at the University of Exeter has shown that taking notes improves one's recall of the material by a factor of six. It's because you're *actively* involved. You're not just sitting there and passively taking things in by listening or reading. If you were to say something out loud *and* write it down, the improvement would be even more dramatic.

Note-taking also forces you to *think*. You have to extract the key ideas, move from the specific to the general, recognise the *intent* of something being said in a certain way ... and so on. It actively *involves* your intellect in what is going on.

> A pictorial representation is better than text at capturing the essence of an idea or concept.

Un-lined paper is for drawing pictures and they are enormously beneficial. A page filled with boxes, arrows, diamonds and wiggly lines – with just a few words of text – can often capture the essence of an idea in a way that words all by themselves just can't match:

- A pictorial representation allows us to show and see the interconnections between things. A simple arrow is all that it takes.
- Pictures are better than words at presenting ideas *holistically.* Words are very much a *linear* or *left-brain* form of expression.
- It allows a lot more information to be summarised on a single sheet of paper. A good 80 per cent of text is 'padding' that does not convey meaning.
- We don't have to flip back and forth between page 17 and page 24 as we struggle to relate one part of an overall concept to another.

Do-It problems

Much of what we have been discussing in this chapter applies to our handling of *Fix-It* problems but less obviously to *Do-It* problems. The latter, as we have discussed, involve the achievement of something. We've been asked to:

- Put together a newsletter.
- Spearhead a fund-raising drive.
- Select a training programme.
- Find a recruiting agency that we can work with.

It's a *problem*, in that (1) there is a gap between where we are now and where we want to be and (2) the strategy and means for closing that gap are indeterminate. But it's a more positive sort of problem, more achievement-oriented, lending itself to a more proactive approach.

And the focus of our data-gathering in Step Two will be as much on the state of affairs that we want to *achieve* as on the way things are at present. Our concern isn't to pinpoint the *cause* of a problem so much as it is to clarify where we want to *get* to – what the *solution* will look like, in other words:

- What sort of newsletter should it be?
- What will be its primary purpose?
- Will distribution be to an internal audience only or will we be sending it out to suppliers and customers as well?
- What sort of resources do we have to work with? How much can we spend?
- Do we have anyone on board who has done this kind of thing before?

Staying with the newsletter example, an appropriate strategy for our total information-gathering stage might include the following:

- Doing some random interviewing to see what employees would like to see in a newsletter.
- Confirming and expanding upon the above findings using a questionnaire survey to all employees.
- Talking to the senior people – about their own expectations.
- Drawing up a few sample pages and getting some reactions.
- Asking for samples of newsletters from our Training & Development catalogue.
- Asking for some technical-type newsletters from next week's trade show in Geneva.

Summary

In this chapter we have looked at the importance of information gathering.

- Rarely will we have time to gather all the information we need about a problem. We need to collect and analyse the *critical* facts.
- It's not enough to just gather facts. We have to understand what they *mean*. The trick is to get *good* information.
- Fact-finding is largely a matter of asking the right questions.
- *What, where, when, who, why* ... these are good words to be using. They keep us looking.
- The best way to gather information about a problem is to get out there and talk to the people involved.
- It is often helpful to solicit individual observations from a few trusted colleagues before getting the whole team together.
- There are many sources of information to tap. *Too* many, in fact. Be selective.
- How we *represent* the facts is crucial. Organise information so that we can see the highlights at a glance.
- A *force-field analysis* is a useful way of identifying the *forces* at work.
- A *SWOT* model forces us to be comprehensive by giving us boxes that have to be filled out.

CHAPTER 5

Defining the Problem

Defining the real problem properly is perhaps the most critical step of all in the problem-solving cycle.
Okay, now we have the facts. What – exactly – is the problem?

Defining a problem is tantamount to *understanding* it. Knowing why it's there and how it is likely to change between now and next week if we leave it alone.

That's the sort of understanding we'll want to reach by the end of this chapter. And, once we've developed that level of clarity about what the problem *is*, we'll probably know what has to be done about it. But unless we get the problem definition step right, any attempt to *solve* the problem is likely to be futile. We may solve the problem by sheer happenstance or brute force, but the chances of that happening two times in a row are slim.

So – what is the *real* problem? That is the question we have to answer.

Identifying the gap

A 'problem', we have said, is a gap between the way things are and the way we *want* them to be – and 'problem-solving' is how we *close* that gap. It follows, therefore, that our goal at this stage is to understand the two sides of the gap – the way things are now and the way they will be once we've solved the problem. Only once we have properly defined that gap do we go on to the next stage in the problem-solving cycle and think about how to bridge it.

It might be useful, indeed, to reproduce our diagram of the problem-solving process and insert it here as Figure 17. We'll do this again from time to time as a way of keeping the model in our mind as we work through the various stages.

Figure 18 takes a close-up look at what goes on during Step 3 of

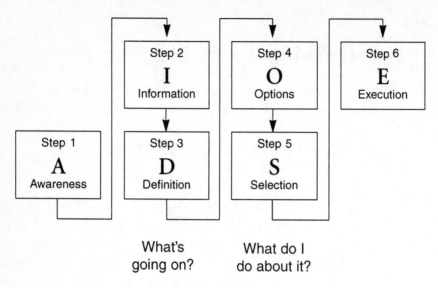

Fig. 17. The AIDOSE model.

the problem-solving cycle. All the information that we gathered during Step 2 is channelled into one of two boxes.

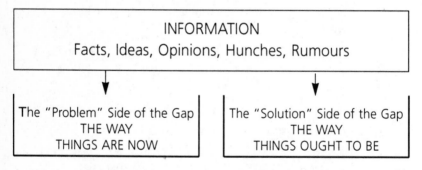

Fig. 18. Close-up of Step 3 of the problem-solving cycle.

- ◆ The box on the left represents the current state of affairs. We can think of the left as being the 'problem' side of the gap.
- ◆ The box on the right is for information about the way things *ought* to be. We can think of this as being the 'solution' side.

Case study: Jill Pritchard

To illustrate how this works, let's take the problem of developing a system for clipping newspapers that Jill Pritchard, one of our *Famous Five*, has brought with her. *What is the current situation?* Here's how Jill described things:

'The current situation is that I have newspaper sections and torn-out pages on the coffee table, in the sideboard drawer, in the bathroom. I'll see something that I think I might be able to use in my column, and I'll just tear the whole page out and put it to one side. But I end up with paper all over the place. And when I sit down to write my column, I know there is good material there, lying around somewhere, but I don't have access to it. Trying to find a specific article is too frustrating. There is a feeling of frustration stemming from the fact that all this potential information and all these potential ideas are going to waste.'

Next, we have to define the other side of the gap – the way things will be once we've solved the problem. As soon as we have described the way things are now we swing right into a description of the way we would like things to be. The reason we do one right after the other is that the two are so closely linked.

Jill:

'How will I know that the problem is solved? I will feel in control of things. Newspaper material will be filed away in some sort of orderly fashion so that I can find or scan things when I need to – either searching for a specific article that I can remember or scanning a topic to see what we have on file. The material will be filed away rather than left lying all around the house the way it is now. The system will be simple to use and using it will give me an absolutely heavenly feeling of being in control of things.' _____

Notice that we're not being terribly specific here. Jill is saying that her clippings will be filed away, but she hasn't specified where or how. That will come later, when we actually move into the *solution* phases of the problem-solving cycle.

How will I know that the problem is solved? That's a useful question to ask when searching for a description of the 'solution' side of the gap. 'What is our objective in this situation?' is just as valid, but doesn't have that natural, down-to-earth ring that we are striving for. Our model – let's keep reminding ourselves – is something that we're actually going to *use*. It has to be natural.

The four boxes – SCOC

Let's go a step further – and sub-divide each of the two boxes in Figure 18 into two. That will give us a total of four boxes, two on each side of the gap, as shown in Figure 19.

On the left, we have two boxes for information about the way things are now – the SYMPTOMS box and the CAUSES box. On the right, we have the two boxes for information about the way things will be once the problem has been solved – the OUTCOMES box and the CONSTRAINTS box.

When we think about the way things are right now our focus will be on separating the symptoms of the problem from the causes. As we shift our attention to the other side of the gap our focus will be on fleshing out the outcomes we want to achieve and the constraints which we have to satisfy in doing so.

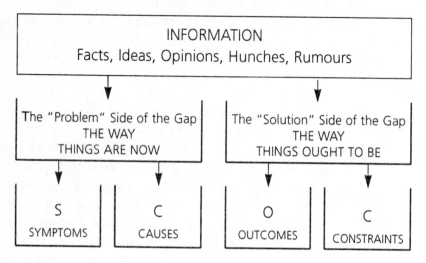

Fig. 19. SCOC model.

Symptoms and causes

The cause of a problem is something that we normally have to *dig* for. Indeed, we often refer to it as the *root* cause.

The use of the unearthing-the-root analogy is a useful reminder that Step 3 of the problem-solving cycle is by no means an easy one. The cause of a problem will not emerge automatically just because we've done a good job, in Step 2, of gathering and organising the facts. *Defining* the problem is something else entirely.

Case study – lagging sales

Let's take a classic *Fix-It* problem. Sales are down. As a regional manager it's our job to do something about it.

Where does the problem occur, and where does it *not* occur? Here, we have to look at sales figures right across the region – and break them down, if we can, into smaller chunks. If the region is *big*, then we can ask ourselves whether the falling off in sales has happened more in one part of the region than in others.

Or maybe it has something to do with sales being hit hard in large urban areas but holding up well in the smaller towns and rural communities. Maybe our sales are down in those areas where our competitor's sales are *up* – and the key to the pattern lies in our *competitor's* sales strategies and figures rather than our own. Maybe there's no pattern at all.

How about the *when* question? When does the problem occur and when does it not occur? Are sales figures down during the first half of the month, climbing in the last week but not enough to offset the lacklustre showing of the first three weeks? Are we being hit hard at any specific point in the year? Do sales improve when I'm away at the annual trade show in Amsterdam?

Who is involved, and who *isn't* involved? Has there been a uniform dip in sales performance right across the team? Is it confined to just a handful of people? Are the poor results being caused by certain *types* of people – people whose training followed a particular pattern, people working under certain managers, people with a certain approach to selling?

What precisely is the problem? What is *not* the problem? Sales are down, yes, but can we be more precise about it? What exactly is down? Sales volume? Profit contribution? If it's sales *volume* that is down then let's be clear about that as well. Has there been an absolute decline in sales, or are we talking about sales falling off just a bit against sales *targets* which have risen quite substantially? Maybe it's just a matter of the competition getting better, and the fault lies with our whole management team for not being aggressive and innovative enough to keep pace. Sales are down, yes, but maybe that's not the problem. Maybe it's the result.

You can see how tricky it gets, even in regard to what appears to be a very straightforward problem. In this specific situation, as it turns out, the *real* problem was eventually defined in the following manner.

Sales are down because our customers – schools, hospitals, and other institutions – are changing their buying habits. Their decisions are being driven increasingly by economic factors, and the decision-making process itself has become increasingly centralised. Buying groups have entered into the mix in a fairly significant way. In those accounts where we have a Key Account Management strategy in place, or where we have a strong performer with a 'consultative' approach to selling, we are doing okay. We are adapting to the changes. Across the board, however, sales are down. We need to take a long, hard look at how the industry is changing and at the implications thereof for our own approach to doing business.

So that's the problem. It's not just the fact that sales are down. That, as it turns out, was just a symptom. The real issue goes a lot deeper and has to do with some rather fundamental questions of change and adaptation and strategy.

Identifying the root cause

There is no single best way of getting down to the root cause of a problem. No single technique that will work in every situation.

Still, there *are* some reasonably specific techniques that we may wish to keep in mind. They won't *replace* the hard work of *thinking* that has to be done at this critical stage of the problem-solving cycle, but they may make it a little bit easier.

Asking why

One way to work toward the root cause of a problem is to keep asking ourselves a simple question – *Why?* – until we run out of answers. Or to have someone else ask.

Bill: I'm having a problem with Jennifer.
Grace: A 'problem' in what sense?
Bill: I just can't seem to work with her.
Grace: Why is that?
Bill: She seems to have a chip on her shoulder.
Grace: Any idea why that is?
Bill: I think – I'm not sure, but I think – she wanted the job over in Marketing that Joanne ended up getting.

Grace: Why is that? Why did she want the job so badly?

Bill: The challenge, I suppose. It's something different. It's a good career move.

Grace: And why should not getting the job cause her to go around with a chip on her shoulder?

Bill: I think she felt she deserved it more than Joanne.

Grace: Why?

Bill: Uh, I'm not sure. I think she just felt that she was better qualified to do the job.

You can see what Grace is doing. She is backing Bill up, level by level, until he runs out of answers. If she's really astute, she might come back with something like this.

> *'For what it's worth, Bill, I think Joanne was the right person for that job. The whole role of marketing has changed so much in the past year, and I don't know that Jennifer has the sort of strategic skills that we were looking for. More to the point, I'm not sure that Jennifer knows that. I think she needs to be helped to understand exactly what was needed in the marketing role, and why – and, as managers, we generally don't do a very good job of educating people along those lines.'*

Asking the 'not' question

When scientists want to isolate and identify the cause of a problem, they often compare an experimental group of subjects with a control group of subjects. Everything about the two groups is identical except for a single condition – the one being explored.

We can set up the same sort of comparison in the way we ask our *where, when, who,* and *what* questions:

- Where does the problem occur?
- Where does it *not* occur?
- When does the problem occur?
- When does it *not* occur?
- Who is involved in the problem situation?
- Who is *not* involved?
- What precisely *is* the problem?
- What is *not* the problem?

If the problem is that the people on Graeme Weir's team are unhappy with the company's overtime policy, then it raises the question – why aren't people on the *other* teams unhappy? Perhaps they are, but haven't said so. Maybe there's only *one* person on Graeme's team who is unhappy but who has been trying to stir up trouble. Maybe it's all a coincidence.

But – maybe there's something about being on Graeme's team that is the root cause of the problem. The evidence is certainly leaning in that direction. We don't jump to any conclusions, but nor do we ignore what the evidence is suggesting to us.

Some more techniques

Asking questions. Asking a series of 'why' questions. Asking the 'not' question. We've introduced these as specific techniques that help us identify the root cause of a problem situation. Let's add on a few more.

Testing our hypotheses

It will be helpful to think of our ideas about the root cause of a problem as being *hypotheses.* Doing so implies that they have to be tested out in some way. *If X is the cause, then Y should hold true.*

If the increase in 'road rage' incidents on the M25 is caused by an increase in the volume of traffic, then we should find a correlation between the frequency of road rage incidents and volume of traffic. If the rather marked decline in our export business is being caused by the sustained strength of the pound, then historical data should show that our export business has been strongest when the pound has been weakest.

Arguing with ourselves

This technique involves introducing a rule – Every time we come up with something that we think is the real cause of the problem, another part of us has to play devil's advocate and try to refute it. In other words, we have to argue with ourselves. Specifically, we have to argue ourselves out of believing that we have indeed got down to the root cause in our attempt to understand the problem.

This is not the cause – and here's proof. That's the sort of statement the devil's advocate side of us will be trying to make.

*If low wages were the cause, the morale problem would be found
on Ward Two and Ward Three as well, not just Ward Four – so,
no, low wages can't be the cause of the problem.*

Taking action – hypothetically

The idea here is to play out a solution in our mind and see
whether it in fact solves the problem. If it bridges the gap between
the way things are and the way we want them to be then we can
conclude that it successfully got at the root cause of the problem.
If the problem persists, then our solution has missed the mark.
But remember – we're doing this all in our *head*. Hypothetically.

If I fix this, will it solve the problem? That's the question we
have to ask ourselves. If the answer is either:

◆ No, it won't.
◆ No, not necessarily.
  – then we should continue our search for the real cause.

If the fall-off in business out of the Dublin office is the result of
poor leadership then appointing a stronger manager should
produce an increase in business. *Would it?* It's difficult to know for
sure but we owe it to ourselves to play the solution out in our
mind and at least make an educated guess. If we can imagine a
new, stronger manager do our instincts tell us that the results
coming out of the Dublin office would demonstrate a significant
improvement?

Why? What would the new manager do, or not do, that would
cause the situation to change?

The point is this. We can't afford to move ahead on the basis of
blind faith. There's too much at stake – in this situation it's not
just the health and welfare of the Dublin office and its customer
base and the good will we've established over the years; it's
people's careers as well. So we have to tread carefully. Unless we
can make a convincing case for the idea that replacing staff will
get at the root cause and hence solve the problem, then we need to
keep working on our definition of the problem.

Drawing a picture

We have talked before about the usefulness of representing
information pictorially. Pictorial representations, we said, are

better than words at showing relationships and capturing the holistic essence of a complex situation.

The very act of *drawing* the picture is often enough to bring the causal relationships in a complex situation out into the open where we can see them. Connecting this box to that box, deciding whether the arrow should face this way ($\rightarrow$) or that way ($\leftarrow$), deciding whether this box represents a people issue or a technical issue ... slowly but surely we begin to get a sense of how things hang together. We begin to *understand* the situation.

Outcomes and constraints

To reiterate:

♦ A problem is a gap between the way things are and the way things ought to be.
♦ Defining a problem means identifying the *symptoms, causes, outcomes,* and *constraints.*

We've talked about *symptoms* and *causes*. Let's turn our attention now to *outcomes* and *constraints*. Outcomes are results which our chosen solution will have to produce. Constraints are limits within which we have to operate. On both fronts, we need to be as clear and specific as we possibly can.

Fix-It versus Do-It problems

There is an important distinction between the two classes of problem that has to do with our whole approach to *defining* the problem.

When we are dealing with a *Fix-It* problem:

♦ The current state of affairs is what constitutes the problem. Something is *wrong* with the way things are.
♦ So we focus on that side of the gap. That's where we have to gather information and do our thinking.
♦ Our aim, ultimately, is to make the problem go away.

When we are dealing with a *Do-It* problem:

♦ Our focus is more on the future side of the gap, the way we would like things to be.
♦ So we focus on fleshing out and thinking about what it is we wish to achieve and why.

◆ Our aim is to *create* or *achieve* the desired state of affairs.

In gathering information and working toward a definition of the problem, in other words:

◆ If it's a *Fix-It* problem, we'll spend most of our time on the *symptoms and causes* side of the gap.

◆ If it's a *Do-It* problem, we'll spend most of our time on the *outcomes and constraints* side.

But the challenge is the same in both cases. We need to understand where we are starting from, and where we want to get to. And the work, as it turns out, is similar in both cases. It involves digging, asking the *Why* question, pushing things back from one level to the next again and again until we arrive at something that has the ring of finality about it.

The real objective

Case Study: Tony Martindale _____

It is important that we take time to define the *real* objective we are trying to achieve. Here's tony Martindale, one of our *Famous Five* and the Director of Sales and Marketing for one of the country's most dynamic packaged foods companies:

> 'One of my people – Susan – had taken it upon herself to create a resource library. It was added to her annual objectives as a one-off goal. At the end of the year, when we were doing her performance appraisal, I raised the issue of the library. Susan was surprised because the library thing was done – an empty office had been converted to a resource room stocked with a good supply of books and magazines and resource material. But I pointed out to Susan that no one was using it. I hadn't seen one person actually go into the library, and it's just down the hall from my office. Was that our objective, I asked Susan – to create a really impressive library that no one uses? Or was the real objective to get our people reading more, or to inject some new ideas into our thinking, or to get people to look at what other companies are doing before they commit us to a course of action? What was the actual outcome that we wanted to achieve, and why was it important? Susan hadn't really stopped to ask herself that question.'

A good example. And a good question to be asking ourselves. *What is the actual outcome that we want to achieve, and why is it important?*

In effect – Why do we need a resource library? That's the question Susan has to ask herself. And the answer might be – *So our people will have ready access to relevant books and journals and internal reports and market data.* But then we ask a follow-up question. And why is that important? *Because we want our people to be making decisions on the basis of the best possible data and intelligence.* And why is that important? *Because the problems they are dealing with are getting more and more complex, the stakes are higher, and the need for up-to-date intelligence is more acute.*

So our objective is to better equip our people to operate effectively in an environment that is becoming increasingly complex and intellectually demanding. Developing a resource library, then, becomes a *strategy* for achieving this outcome.

And recognising this is useful. The person who is out to develop a resource library is going to do things one way. The person who is out to better equip our people to deal with an increasingly complex environment will do things in another. Their respective mindsets will have a very real bearing on the way they approach the project. _____

Constraints

Develop a resource library and:

- Have it done by the end of the month.
- Don't spend more than £1,000.
- Don't knock any walls down.
- Convert a spare office.
- Get Bill to help out with wiring and lighting if necessary.

These are some simple constraints imposed upon a comparatively simple project, and we are using them to illustrate the nature of 'constraints' – as distinct from 'outcomes'. Constraints are limits within which we have to operate. They are limits in terms of five main resources:

- Time
- Space
- Money
- Materials
- People.

Constraints may also involve limits on the range of solutions that will be deemed acceptable – a minimum level of results or the need to operate within certain strategic or policy boundary lines.

◆ The solution, for example, has to be acceptable to the directors because it needs their approval.
◆ The projected increase in profit contribution should be at least 15 per cent.
◆ The design of the product has to be consistent with standards being introduced by our US parent.
◆ The project should capitalise on our unique status as a full-range supplier.
◆ It should not commit us to any arrangement that runs longer than eighteen months.

Summary

In this chapter we looked at the critical step of defining the problem.

◆ Defining a problem is tantamount to *understanding* it. Knowing why it is there and how it is likely to change if we leave it alone.
◆ And, once we've developed that level of clarity about what the problem *is*, we will probably know what has to be done about it.
◆ Unless we get the problem definition step right, any attempt to *solve* the problem is likely to be futile.
◆ Our goal at this stage is to articulate and understand the two sides of the gap.
◆ On the way-things-are-now side of the gap, we need to gather information about, and identify, the *symptoms* and the *causes* of the problem.
◆ On the way-things-ought-to-be side of the gap, we need to think about, and identify, the *outcomes* to be achieved and the *constraints* to be met.
◆ There is no single best way of getting down to the root cause of a problem.
◆ One way to work toward the root cause of a problem is to keep asking ourselves a simple question – *Why?* – until we run out of answers.
◆ It will be helpful to think of our ideas about the root cause of a problem as being *hypotheses* which need to be tested out in some way.
◆ The most common way to test an hypothesis is through the simple application of logic. *If X is the cause, then Y should hold true.*

- ◆ Outcomes are results which our chosen solution will have to produce. Constraints are limits within which we have to operate.
- ◆ If our problem is a *Fix-It* problem, we'll spend most of our Step 2 and Step 3 time on the *symptoms and causes* side of the gap.
- ◆ If our problem is a *Do-It* problem, we'll spend most of our Step 2 and Step 3 time on the *outcomes and constraints* side of the gap.
- ◆ But the challenge is the same in both cases. We need to understand where we are starting from, and where we want to go.

CHAPTER 6

Developing Solution Options

We've gathered the facts. We know what the problem is. We're committed to solving it. The question facing us now is ... What are our options?

At this point, then, we've defined the problem as a gap between the way things are and the way things ought to be. Now ... we're ready to move on to that of the problem-solving cycle – Steps 4 through 6 – where the *solution*, not the problem, takes the spotlight.

The solution will usually not be obvious. If it were, someone would surely have implemented it by now and solved the problem. So we have more hard work ahead of us – and the quality of the solution we select will only be as good as the range of options we generate and examine.

Some guidelines to keep in mind

We're looking for ways to bridge the gap. We don't have to narrow things down to a single best solution – that will be done in the next Step of the cycle. What we want to do is simply make sure that every solution worth looking at has been put on the table.

Let's give some thought to five guidelines that will help us do precisely that.

1. Focus on feasibility

The solution of a problem rarely, if ever, calls upon us to consider every single option. If the problem is something as mundane as choosing a vacation spot, it seems obvious that we won't give active consideration to every single vacation spot in the *world* before making our final choice. There is, instead, a much narrower range of options within which we conduct our search – places we have been to before, or which have been recommended to us by friends, or which have come to our attention through a television programme or a newspaper article. If our problem is that of poor morale on the factory floor, sacking the director of manufacturing may not be an option that we give a lot of thought to even though it might make sense.

So we're looking for options which promise to deliver the outcomes we have targeted and satisfy the constraints within which we are operating.

The example supplied by Tony Martindale in the last chapter is a clear illustration of how constraints place limits on the range of solutions we can consider. A computerised storage system would be nice, but if there's a £1,000 cap on spending then it's hardly worth a second thought. A *large* reference library, combining Jack's old office with the one that Nancy is in, with Nancy moving down the hall to team up with Frances, is also not worth spending time on because we've been told that we have to operate within the existing office layout. No knocking down of walls.

2. Boil it down to alternatives

Once we have moved from all those options which are *possible* to considering only those which are *feasible*, we'll still have our hands full. As house-hunters, let's say, we've gone from considering – in theory at least – every house in the Windsor to Maidenhead area to considering only those which have three bedrooms and are within a certain price range.

We still have to carry the process of elimination further. On the assumption that it's usually easier to *reject* things than *include* them, we scan the remaining options and look for something that we can use to throw a few of them out or put them on the back burner where further consideration is doubtful.

Ideally, we would like to narrow it down to a choice between two options. Two candidates for a job. Two possible sites for the new distribution centre. It might be three. It could be four. But once we get to five, making a decision starts to become difficult. Two makes for a nice, natural decision. Three is probably the practical limit.

3. *Don't neglect the do-nothing option*

Deciding not to decide is always an option. You can leave the problem unsolved on the assumption that – if left alone – it will solve itself. Or, it might be a timing issue; the problem has to be solved, but now is not the best time to do it. An example of this is the strategy adopted by both John Major's Tory government and its Labour successor – of seeking to be *involved* in shaping and influencing the development of the European Union without making a firm commitment to formal entry. This is the do-nothing option, under the guise of keeping one's options open until such time as a decision either *has* to be made or can be made on the basis of better information.

So, in thinking about solution options, we have to ask the question – Do we need to take action at all? Will the situation resolve itself if we leave well enough alone? Is there a chance that we'll make things *worse* by meddling? Are there simply more *important* things that we should be getting on with.

There's a rule of thumb that we should be very clear about.

> Never choose the do-nothing option simply because you can't think of anything better to do; choose it for a specific reason which you can articulate.

The Bank of England may choose to do nothing about recessionary pressures on British industry because its focus is on the long-term control of inflation. A managing director may choose to do nothing about a lack of new products on the horizon because the business plan is to grow primarily through acquisition over the next two years.

What we're calling the 'do-nothing' option doesn't always mean doing nothing in the literal sense of the word. Beyond doing nothing at all, there are several very legitimate ways of making less than a full decision about the problem you are dealing with.

- ◆ Monitor the situation: If the problem is not an urgent one, if it appears to be stable rather than getting worse, then a decision to simply monitor the situation is certainly justifiable.
- ◆ Treat the symptoms: Do this when the symptoms are troublesome and demand an urgent response even though a tackling of the underlying cause is going to have to wait or can simply not be done quickly.

- Make a temporary decision: Do something quickly, but make it a temporising move designed to buy time. It allows you to move quickly without committing yourself to a 'hard' decision.
- Make a conditional decision: Make the decision but stop short of moving on to the implementation stage until the timing is right or the decision is needed. You're prepared to act quickly when the time comes. That's the key thing.

4. Try to think 'outside the box'

Let's just talk briefly about what creativity is – and its role in the whole problem-solving process.

At the risk of dragging out a time-worn example, let's think briefly about the joining-the-dots problem from which stems the creative thinking known as 'thinking outside the box'. The problem is simple. You have to join all the dots in a 3 × 3 matrix using only three lines. The solution involves quite literally *thinking outside the box*.

Thinking outside the box means – *I wouldn't have thought of that*. It means that the answer is somehow outside the range of solutions we would have considered.

And *why* is it outside? Because it breaks a rule we've been following in our thinking. In the case of the nine-dots problem we believe that our straight lines can't extend beyond the box formed by the nine dots. No one has specified that that is a rule. We've just *assumed* it.

The key point is this – creativity isn't just a matter of brainstorming, and coming up with a lot of wild ideas. It also means releasing our mind from the shackles and boundaries which keep it from wandering too far afield. Questioning our assumptions means asking questions which, at first blush, seem a bit too 'obvious' to be worth asking. For example:

- Is this problem worth solving?
- Is it really a 'problem'?
- What if we just told them the truth?
- What if we just forgot about the whole thing and went back to work?
- What if we just went ahead and launched the product anyway?

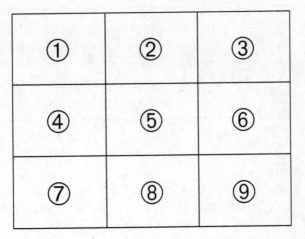

Fig. 20. The nine dot problem.

5. *Look for the logic in the situation*

In most situations, *clear* thinking is more important than *creative* thinking when it comes to solving a problem.

> *If the main issue is that the customer doesn't like dealing with four or five different sales reps, each handling a different product area, then it makes sense to think in terms of having a major account executive serving as our single point of contact.*

The structure of this statement is critical. *If* the main issue or the key to this whole problem is this or that ... *then it makes sense to think in terms of* taking this or that approach to dealing with it.

Addressing the main issue is a good example of thinking *logically* about a problem, and allowing the logic inherent in the problem situation itself to suggest the appropriate solution.

We talked about this when we discussed the search for the root cause of a problem – if you can put your finger on the *nub* of the problem, the *solution* to the problem will generally become quite obvious. That doesn't make problem-solving *easy*. It just means that the *real* challenge is identifying the nub of the problem – not coming up with ten creative ways of solving it.

If the main issue is	then it makes sense to think in terms of
that our support staff don't take the spending guidelines *seriously* enough ...	doing something tangible to drive home the point that we really mean business.
the lack of communication between the Engineering and Logistics people ...	breaking down the barrier between these groups before we do anything else.
the *packaging* of the idea, rather than its content per se or the logic behind it ...	bringing in a marketing expert rather than spending more money on the design consultants.

Fig. 21. Logical thinking.

Some good questions to ask

Now let's look at some useful *questions* which will perform the same function ... to help ensure, before we go on, that every solution worth looking at has been put on the table.

1. *What did we do the last time?*

If the problem we're facing has occurred before, and if what we did the last time to solve the problem seemed to do the trick, let's not jump to the conclusion that we should do exactly the same thing again. Let's at least put that solution on our list of options to be considered.

But let's also keep the following points in mind:

- The two situations may *look* the same but contain some very subtle differences.
- Because of the *timing* issue, what worked last time may not work as well this time.
- There's always a chance that we chose the *wrong* solution last time – but it just happened to work.
- There's a *good* chance that what we did last time was an adequate solution but not an optimal one.

2. *What did our competitors do?*

We're being hit hard by smaller and more nimble competitors

coming in with me-too products. That's the problem we have to explore, analyse, define, and solve.

If our major competitors have faced the same problem, then it makes sense to find out as much as we can about what they did to solve it and why. There's bound to be something we can learn from a study of what counter-strategies they used and what sort of results they were able to achieve.

But we'll need to be geared up for this type of intelligence-gathering. If we don't have someone on staff clipping newspaper articles on our chief competitors and on comparable companies in other industries, then we should have. If none of us has a good contact in the competitor's camp, then we've got to find a way to develop one.

3. Will this actually solve the problem?

Options have to be *explored* – not just identified. It is worth taking a few minutes to think each one through.

What this does is bring the option *to life*. It translates the *idea* of doing something into an action-based *reality* that we can see and touch and feel. And that, in turn, helps us more properly evaluate just what the option will do for us in practise. What outcomes it will produce. What obstacles will have to be overcome. How long things will take, and what can go wrong at each step along the way.

The most common pitfalls

As we did in our discussion of the Problem Awareness stage of the problem-solving cycle, let's systematically go through some of the most common pitfalls at that point in the cycle when our attention turns to the development of solution options. Three stand out.

1. Not considering all the options

The most common mistake that we tend to make isn't that of making the *wrong* selection from the alternate courses of action that we are considering. Rather, it's the failure to put a full range of alternatives on the table for consideration.

The real culprit, in most cases, is an undue emphasis on the act of decision-making as distinct from the process of problem-solving. We seem to forget that information-gathering and thinking are just as legitimate as the more glamorous and attention-getting act of making a decision.

2. Searching for the 'right' solution

It is going to be very difficult if we worry too much about finding the *right* solution. If we delay the moment of decision until we have found the *right* product to launch or the *right* person to marry … then the chances of us ever making a decision at all are slim.

What we need to look for are solutions that will work. Solutions that will deliver the goods, get the job done, or in some cases just allow us to move on to something else. They don't have to be perfect. They just have to be good, workable, manageable solutions.

3. Sticking with the tried and true

Settling for too little. That's what this pitfall is all about. Settling for the safe, predictable, boring range of options when something a lot more exciting and *effective* is really what the situation is crying out for.

Maybe 'crying out for' is a bit too strong. It implies that we're ignoring a blatant call for creativity by putting on our blinkers. We're not. It's just that we're operating under pressure. We have a lot of things to do. Why not save our creativity, and the *time* it takes to be creative, for those situations where we are truly stymied and have to come up with something new and different?

Thinking strategically

Case Study: Jack Carter _____

Too often, we move from goal-setting to action-taking without stopping to develop a general strategy. Insertion of a strategic step into the problem-solving cycle is one of the most beneficial things we can do in working to become a more effective problem-solver.

Let's listen in as Jack talks about his approach to one of the country's leading supermarket chains – specifically his effort to win the chain's total own-brand business away from the competition.

'It's taken the better part of a year-and-a-half, getting them to the point where we're now talking about us supplying their own-brand school supplies

and household stationery items. For the first two months I kept hammering away at this person and then that person, telling them how great our products were and how we could bring their costs down and all the usual things that I am sure they hear from every potential supplier.

It was only after two months of flailing around that Frank, my manager, told me to take a few days off and develop a proper business plan. He used the idea of "thinking backwards" ... starting out by visualising the end result I wanted to achieve and then working backward to see how I got there. And he emphasised the fact that the strategy had to be right. The overall approach. That was the secret.'

Thinking backwards. Thinking strategically. Let's see if we can't find out exactly what Jack's boss was getting at. It seems, from what Jack has said so far, to have produced results.

A lot of us, when faced with a problem, are inclined to skip over a very important step. We leap from the *goal* to the *action plan*. Some of us jump right into action. Others clearly *plan*, but it's *action* planning ... deciding what steps we're going to take.

What we're skipping over is the development of a *strategy*. A general approach, in other words. Most significant goals can be pursued by using more than one overall approach.

Here's Jack again:

'To land a new account, or get an existing customer to take on a new product, there are several different strategies I can use. I can go in there aggressively and trust that my own confidence and enthusiasm and leadership – backed by my company's track record for quality products – will be enough to produce a positive decision on their part. Or, I can put together a comprehensive financial analysis that lays out current and projected costs and benefits. One of our accounting people can handle the gathering of data and we probably have some presentation software that will allow us to put our case forward in a convincing fashion.'

And so on. That's what we mean by 'strategy'. It means defining the space within which our solution will be developed or searched for. Strategies, therefore, exist on a more general or abstract level than 'solutions'. And the practical reason for thinking strategically *before* we give consideration to specific solution options is that it (1) cuts down on the amount of work we have to do and (2) increases the likelihood of our getting things right.

It cuts down on the amount of work

We're going on holiday. I've decided that. So we're going to set a week aside and go to Jersey. Or Cornwall. Or the Lake District. Somewhere really nice and relaxing.

Having resolved that, I am left with a problem to solve. The problem is that of deciding where to go, and then making the arrangements. Like any other problem, it will mean laying out as many options as possible, weighing their respective pros and cons, narrowing it down to the two best options, choosing one, and then making the final arrangements.

I have a box of travel brochures at home, and there's a tourist office not too far from here where I can get a lot more. Plus, I've been saving newspaper clippings about exotic places to visit for *years* now. I'll get the Travel section from the *Sunday Times* and the *Daily Mail* and look at the special deals they have on for this month and next …

That's me. Moving into action. Getting *busy*. Being something of a collector by inclination I *do* have lots of travel ideas stored away in my files. And my first impulse is to both (1) get them out and (2) get *more*.

But I'm going to stop myself this time. I'm *not* going to invest five or six hours going through piles of newspaper clippings and magazine articles.

No, I'm going to think *strategically* and ask *What sort of vacation do we want, and what's the best way to go about deciding where we want to go?*

The answer then comes with surprising ease and clarity. We want a relaxing *family* vacation, and the best way to decide where to go is to talk about it as a family over supper tonight. We can give ourselves a few days to think and talk about it, and maybe plan on making a final decision by the end of the weekend.

So – I'm *not* going to take over in my usual way. I'm not going to turn the house upside down with little piles of newspaper clippings – one for the *Greek Islands*, one for *Mauritius*, one for *Scotland* – covering every piece of furniture that doesn't already have a plant on it.

No, the important thing is that it be a *family* vacation … a *relaxing* family vacation. Clarifying that – stopping to *think* about it – takes hardly a minute. But it can cut out *hours* of work. It *addresses* the whole question of strategy. Not *Where do we go for our vacation?* but *What's the best way to decide?*

It helps us get things right

Thinking strategically also helps us get things right. There's less likelihood of spending days and days working to implement a solution and then finding that we've been barking up the wrong tree.

Do we need a *quick* solution or an *optimal* solution? Do we want to talk 'partnership' with them or threaten to take them to court? Do I try to work *with* the school or will I get better results by taking an *adversarial* approach? Is this just an interesting idea or a bona fide *opportunity* that needs to be taken seriously and explored further?

These are *strategic* questions. They are invitations to choose a general *class* or *category* of solution before looking at specific options.

Developing a single option

You might be a bit worried at this stage. What's all this about developing a range of options, you might be asking; Hell, I'm having trouble even coming up with one.

> Managers don't always generate a range of solutions. They struggle with the problem and, slowly but surely, they start to settle on and build and sculpture a solution.

Don't fret. Jack Carter, one of our *Famous Five*, had this to say:

'In most situations, I don't think the idea of lining up a whole range of options is realistic. At least it doesn't describe the way things happen in my own experience. Most of my time is spent developing and testing out and refining a single solution. Why try to think of five ways to solve a problem when it only takes one good solution? So I'm asking myself all the time – How am I going to solve this thing? What's the best thing to do?'

What Jack is telling us, in effect, is that managers don't always generate a *range* of solutions. They struggle with the problem and turn it over in their minds, and look for the best way to tackle it. And, slowly but surely, they start to settle on and build and sculpture a solution. It takes shape slowly, with a lot of re-working and testing out and refining going on along the way. But it's all one solution – continually evolving and changing shape, yes, but still one single solution.

Summary

In this chapter we looked at how we arrive at the best range of solutions.

- Our goal in Step 4 is not to *choose* a solution. It is simply to make sure that every solution worth looking at has been put on the table.
- The solution will usually not be obvious. If it were, someone would surely have implemented it by now.
- We are looking for options which are *feasible* within the limits of the situation and using the resources at our disposal.
- Ideally, we would like to narrow it down to a choice between two options.
- Deciding not to decide is always an option.
- Choose the do-nothing option for a specific reason which you can articulate.
- Creativity means 'thinking outside the box'.
- Thinking strategically is an important part of the problem-solving process.
- Not considering all the options is one of the most common pitfalls at this stage.
- In practise, we won't always generate a *range* of options. We may spend our time building and fine-tuning what is in effect a single option.

CHAPTER 7

Choosing the Best Solution

I t's time, now, to decide – to settle on the best and most workable way to bridge the gap between the way things are and the way we want them to be. We've laid out a series of options and the task now is to choose the best one.

Best doesn't mean scientifically best or logically best or theoretically best. It means practically and realistically best in terms of its impact on the real world. So it is here that such elements as judgement, business sense and intuition come into play.

Our goal in this chapter is to make you *really good* at choosing the best option. We want word to get around that you've got a special sense that allows you to go with the option which – though less appealing at first blush – turns out to be right on the money.

An effective decision

Knowing whether a decision is good, bad, or in-between is not as simple or as straightforward as it might seem. Ultimately, the test of our decision is whether or not it solves the problem. An *effective* decision, or an effective solution, is one which accomplishes the intended result.

In practise, we generally aren't in a position to *see* the results of our choice until well after it has been made and implemented. So the question becomes – *What specific things, if we do them, will help ensure that our chosen solution to go with turns out to be an effective one?*

There are several strategies. All will apply to most problem-solving situations. All can and should be used concurrently:

- Get the process right.
- Test out the decision – mentally.
- Test out the decision – in practise.
- Put it in words.
- Get the right people involved.
- Assess and cover the risks.
- Get the timing right.
- Don't let decisions become rules.

Get the process right

Bad decisions are rarely the result of poor decision-making in the sense that the problem-solver just doesn't know how to make a good decision. No, bad decisions are much more likely to occur because of a weakness in another part of the problem-solving cycle. The problem was improperly defined. Or, our information-gathering efforts were inadequate.

There are *so* many places where just a slight oversight can throw the whole process off and result in our choosing a solution which turns out to be sub-optimal.

> Let's make sure we get the process right. That is a mantra that we should be repeating to ourselves over and over again until we get sick of hearing it.

Test out the decision – mentally

There are times when it is helpful to sketch out a rough plan for *implementing* the solution as a means of helping us make the actual decision to go ahead with it. Sketching out an action plan focuses our mind on the practical details – the resources we will need, the timing, the people whose involvement or co-operation will be required, and so on. It's a good way, too, to look at the risks that might be involved – the things that could go wrong, the problems that might be *caused* by our solution and need to be addressed and dealt with along the way. In effect, it's a good way to *test out* our solution before committing ourselves to it.

And – what happens if something goes wrong? Have we allowed for enough leeway in our time estimates to deal with obstacles and setbacks? If there is a price increase, if Joe isn't available to do the programming until later in the month ... can we still get the thing done and get it done by the deadline date?

Test out the decision – in practice

Some decisions lend themselves to an actual testing process, and when that is the case it should be taken advantage of.

- Putting a new control system in place in one part of the factory to assess how well it works.
- Having a sampling of users in three departments try out a new software programme for one week.
- Putting a merchandising display unit in a handful of stores to see how customers react.
- Doing a mock-up of the newsletter and asking a dozen or so employees to read and critique it.
- Delegating the problem to Customer Service this one time, to see whether they can handle it.

At other times, 'testing' a decision involves trying it out on one or two key people before taking it to the group as a whole. This is important in situations where the decision needs to be vetted or approved by other people – the board of directors, for example.

When we can test the waters ahead of time with one or two people, it allows us to get a 'feel' for how the group is likely to react in general. And that makes us more confident of coming away with what we want.

Put it in words

Never make a decision without going through it with at least one other person. In other words – never make a decision in isolation. The mere fact of putting your thoughts and intentions into *words* is one of the surest and most reliable aides to straight thinking.

Get the right people involved

We'll be talking about getting people involved in *implementing* the solution – but it is equally important that the right people be involved in actually *selecting* the best solution.

For one thing, their knowledge, experience and expertise may be needed. If there's a question about costs, or a programming issue, or a need to see whether something is feasible from a logistics standpoint – then we need someone at the table who can provide a sound, authoritative answer or know how to go about finding one.

Beyond that, of course, there is the whole issue of ownership and commitment. If we're counting on people to run with the ball or get their respective teams on board, then we'll want to make sure that they all feel pretty good about the decision we've made. We'll want them to actually feel a sense of commitment to it and to have some sort of *stake* in its successful implementation. And for that, of course, they have to be involved.

And ... the earlier on in the problem-solving process the better.

Really think this one through carefully. Whose commitment will be essential? Whose input will be needed? And when, exactly, should these people be brought into the loop?

Assess and cover the risks

> There is an element of risk in most decision-making situations, and we need to be as clear as we can about what risks we are incurring and how those risks can be minimised.

Our chosen solution will be one which, in our estimation, represents the best possible balance between beneficial outcomes and potential disadvantages. But we can never be sure that the solution we have so carefully chosen will actually do the job. There will always be a risk that it will either allow the problem to linger on or produce some sort of untoward side-effect.

So – there is an element of *risk* in most decision-making situations, and we need to identify the risks and decide how they can be minimised. It means asking, and answering, a few basic questions:

♦ What can go wrong?
♦ What are the chances of that happening?
♦ How serious would the consequences be?
♦ What steps would we take to deal with them?
♦ Can we reduce the likelihood of it happening?
♦ What is the *worst* possible thing that could happen?
♦ Are we prepared to live with that?

What's the worst thing that can happen? That's an especially useful question, and it's always best to answer it in some detail. And then – *Are we prepared to live with it?* If you are charged with making an important stock-market investment decision, for example, you have to know that you or your client can live with the consequences of an unfortunate turn of events. You make the investment. The stock plummets in value for reasons which could not have been foreseen. *Can you or your client absorb the worst-case-scenario loss?* That's the issue.

Get the timing right

As things move more quickly, we have to respond more quickly. It's not so much that *decisions* themselves need to be made more quickly; It's that the problem-solving process has to be more attuned to what is happening on almost a day-to-day basis.

- We can't afford to get bogged down in data analysis. If the computer can do it, let the computer do it.
- Intelligence – knowing what is going on – is crucial. The manager has to know what is happening.
- We have to keep a close eye on what is happening *outside* our organisation, in the industry at large.
- There is no room for procrastination. The cost of delay is getting higher and higher all the time.

Sometimes, yes, our decisions will have to be made more quickly. And that is because they have to keep pace with the increased cost of delay. If delay means being *third* on the market with a new product or concept, rather than first, the cost is incalculably high.

But the key point is that the problem-solving cycle as a whole has to be more aligned with the sheer *speed* with which things happen and change. Our awareness of potential problems, our intelligence-gathering, our ability to marshal resources and point them at the right target – all these capabilities have to be sharper, crisper, keener, and more effective now than ever before.

Don't let decisions become rules

Decisions have a way of becoming rules if we allow them to. What starts out as a solution to a problem – *How do we get this package to its recipient by noontime tomorrow despite having missed the daily pick-up at the post office?* – becomes a routine solution that we fall back on any time the problem arises.

Some solutions deserve to be routinised, and the above is a good example. There is no point in re-inventing the wheel if we don't have to. We said this back in Chapter 2 – every time we routinise a solution, it's one less decision we have to make.

The trouble begins when we routinise things that shouldn't be routinised. When we handle a problem this week the same way we did last week, without really asking ourselves whether it's the right or the best or the optimal way to do things. When we allow *routines* to become a substitute for *thinking*.

Deciding how to decide

It is often useful to articulate the general *strategy* we will use for making a decision. A hiring decision, for example:

- We're going to hire the first candidate who can do the job. There's a job to be filled, and the key thing is to get someone in there quickly.
- I want the best possible person for the job. If I have to talk to fifty people, I'll do that. If I have to reject them all and start over, I'll do that as well.
- It's attitude I'm after – enthusiasm, desire, commitment. That's what I look for. The technical side of things is something we can teach.
- I won't hire anyone who doesn't have the potential to do the next job and the job after that. I've got to see evidence of growth potential.

These are four different ways of approaching the hiring situation, and each will put its stamp on what sort of person is ultimately hired. It's difficult to argue that one strategy is better than another. The point to be made is simply that they are quite different.

The usefulness of articulating the strategy we are using is that we make it *conscious*. We *decide* to use it rather than allowing it to operate in the background without our awareness.

> Anything that affects the way we solve a problem should be made consciously rather than being allowed to operate unconsciously. That's the rule and it's difficult to argue with it.

Taking the logical route

Case study: Graeme Weir _____

Graeme Weir, one of our *Famous Five*, was quite candid in assessing himself as a decision-maker.

> *'I'm not a quick decision-maker, and I don't like being in situations where I feel pressured to make a quick decision. I guess it's the Engineer in me – I like to have time to sift through the facts and look at the various options and weigh the pros and cons and not move ahead until I'm pretty sure of my ground. That's just the way I am, and I've got to say that I've been pretty successful over the years operating that way. But making snap decisions? Putting out fires? No, that's not something that I'm especially good at.'*

How does Graeme actually make decisions?

> *'I tend to be quite logical about most things. Again, I think what you're seeing is the effect of my training as an Engineer. If I can quantify something – assign values – I will. I do it because it's a good way to discipline the mind, even in situations like hiring where the factors and criteria are relatively loose and subjective.'*

There are three young candidates being assessed for a starting-out role in the operations area. Graeme starts by pulling out a piece of paper – we've reproduced it here as Figure 22 – and pointing to the right-hand column.

> *'I look at six main things – the quality and relevance of their education, the extent to which they have practised what I call continuous learning on their own time, their ability to relate to people and work on a team, their brightness in the interview and in solving various problems during the assessment, their knowledge of our business, and their attitude.'*

He continues:

> *'These, if you like, are the criteria. And I've given each one a value – in the V column – according to how important I think it is as a factor affecting the decision. On a scale from 1 to 3, I've rated Attitude a 3 because it's the one thing I can't teach or train into someone. They have to bring it in with them. Things like Education and Knowledge get a 1 – which means that they are important but I'm willing to make a deal.'*

	V	Larkin		Jones		Stevens	
		R	VR	R	VR	R	VR
Education	1	3	3	3	3	2	2
Learning	2	2	4	1	2	1	2
People Skills	2	1	2	2	4	1	2
Brightness	2	3	6	2	4	2	4
Knowledge	1	2	2	3	3	2	2
Attitude	3	2	6	3	9	2	6
TOTAL			23		25		18

Fig. 22. Decision Matrix.

So there are six *criteria*. Six things that are important. And we've assigned a value to each. Then we turn our attention to the candidates:

> *'I rate each candidate on each criterion. Again, I keep it simple – a rating from 1 to 3, recorded in the R column. Then I multiply the value of V by the value of R. The importance of the criterion times the likelihood that the candidate will satisfy that criterion. Then, when I've done all that, I simply add up the figures in the VR column to get an overall score for each candidate.'*

Formally, what Graeme is describing to us here is called a *Decision Matrix*. It involves listing the criteria that a solution has to satisfy, attaching a value to the importance of each, listing our solutions, attaching a value to the likelihood of each solution satisfying each of our criteria, and then multiplying the various figures together to tell us what each of our three solutions is 'worth' in total. _____

Relying on our instincts

The other way to make a decision is to fill out something like a Decision Matrix, as we have just done. But then we go for a long walk in the park.

We chew on the data and then we trust our instincts.

Let's look at an example.

Case study: Jack Carter _____

Jack Carter, another one of our *Famous Five*, was facing a tough decision not unlike the one that Graeme Weir had to deal with. A key hiring decision. Three top-calibre candidates, all of whom seemed eminently capable of doing the job and delivering above-average performance.

The approach that Jack took to the decision, however, could not have been more different.

> *'I've learned to trust my instincts in a situation like this. No matter how much information you gather about a candidate, no matter how many hours you spend interviewing, no matter how many referees you speak to, it still boils down to a gut feel decision once you narrow things down to the top three or four candidates. I won't hire anyone unless I'm excited about getting them on board and turning them loose.'*

Is there a conflict between this willingness to trust one's instincts and the much more structured and quantitative approach that we saw in Graeme Weir? We asked Jack that question.

> *'Most often, my instincts just confirm what the facts are telling me. But there are times, yes, when I've got to go with the one or the other – and, when that happens, I generally go with what my instincts are telling me. On those occasions when I haven't, I've paid the price every time. When I've trusted my gut feel – my decision to hire Susan Beal is a good example – it has almost always worked out well.'*

Susan Beal?

> *'Her background was all wrong. If I had been using an agency or a recruiting firm, Susan would never have come to my attention. She didn't have any industry experience, she was light in terms of management experience, and her exposure to our type of organisational structure was virtually nil. But there was something about her CV that caught my attention. The fact that she had taken a shot at setting up her own business and won a major contract with BAT. The year she spent working as a special assistant to the Chairman when she was with Northbridge. Her involvement in the AT&T deal. I looked at what she had actually done – as opposed to the job titles she had had – and I thought to myself "Boy, this is an Achiever!". So I had her come in for an interview. And ten minutes after she walked into my office, I knew my instincts had been right. Now, two months later, I'm more convinced than ever.'* _____

Trusting our instincts means letting our mental computer chew on the data we've fed it and then tell us what to do. Is that really the way it works?

Yes. There's a little black box inside us somewhere that functions very much like a computer. Its judgement is based on an internal computation which goes on without our conscious awareness. The end result is that we know, instinctively, how something sits with us.

It's not important that we know *why* we are leaning this way or that way – unless, of course, we have to explain it to the members of the executive committee. What *is* important is that we recognise this side of the way the human organism works and that we learn to trust its output.

A final word from Jack Carter:

> *'I don't want it to sound as if I'm pulling decisions out of a hat, because I'm not. I do think about things, and I try to be quite systematic about it. But, at the end of the day, when I have to total up my thoughts and make an overall decision, I would rather go for a walk in the park than sit at my desk and add up a bunch of figures. Walking through the park, I get a sense of which direction I'm leaning in – and I've learned to pay attention to that sense and trust it. Sitting at a desk, all I've got is a bunch of figures. And, to me, decision-making at this level isn't about adding up figures; it's about judgement.'*

Pitfalls at the solution selection stage

Deciding without deciding.

The non-decision:

Jane: *You should probably let Bill know that we're thinking of re-activating the idea. He may want to sit in on the Tuesday meeting.*
Harry: *Yeah, I suppose so. I'll think about it.*

We probably do this more than we realise. All of us. We make decisions by not making decisions. At the risk of belabouring the obvious, a decision *not* to decide is still a decision. And it won't stop other people from making *their* decisions. The world will keep turning, opportunities will come and go, and the *impact of* our decision-less decision will make itself felt. But by that time, the matter will be out of our hands. Our chance to be proactive, to make a difference, will have come and gone.

Regarding a decision as 'final'

Another common pitfall is that of closing off the entire problem-solving cycle. On the assumption, presumably, that a decision has been made.

The problem, of course, is that we live in a very fluid world, where nothing stands still for very long. A decision that looked good last week may start to show some worrisome tension lines this week. With our attention diverted elsewhere, those tension lines may turn into cracks and we may end up with a worse problem on our hands than we started with.

Some of us still feel that changing our mind is a sign of weakness. We call it indecisiveness and compare it unfavourably with the stolid determination of the more 'decisive' problem-solver whose decision is 'final'. In a more static world, perhaps, this whole view might have some basis for legitimacy. But not today. With all the talk about continuous change and personal development ... surely the need to treat decisions as open-ended and subject to constant review should be obvious. What we have to do is recognise that the effective solution is one that delivers the desired outcomes and meets the relevant constraints. Whether it will stand up equally well next week, or next month – we can't be sure. We'll just have to keep an eye on things and be prepared to re-activate the whole problem-solving cycle if the need to do so is there. What we can *not* do is paste the label 'final' on this or any other solution we come up with.

Waiting until all the facts are in

The problem is, of course, that things change so rapidly these days that by the time the *last* facts come in, the *first* facts will probably have been rendered obsolete.

Plus – there's an assumption being made that having all the facts at our disposal will somehow tell us what to *do* about a problem. The unvoiced corollary to this assumption, of course, is that we won't have to *think* about it or make any *decisions* or exercise any *judgement* or use our *initiative*. The 'facts' will make the decision for us. We'll be off the hook.

Things don't happen that way. And the *cost* of gathering every last scrap of information about a problem would be prohibitive. It would outweigh the value of the decision being made.

Relying too much on 'gut feel'

There's a time, a place and a proper role for instincts and intuition in the problem-solving process. Indeed, it is probably better to err on the side of being *too* reliant on intuition than not reliant *enough*. But, like drinking our two glasses of red wine every day to ward off heart disease, we don't want to carry a good thing too far.

The manager who boasts about having a 'hunch' that is providing the direction to an important decision is suspect. Their leadership should not be followed without a considerable degree of trepidation and vigilance.

The troublesome words are 'boasts' and 'hunch'. Trusting our instincts isn't something we should boast about or do with conviction. It is something we should do cautiously, prudently, and humbly.

Not looking at the big picture

Tunnel vision. That's the problem here. Choosing an option that quite adequately satisfies the local or immediate criteria but falls short when weighed against the demands or constraints of the wider and longer-term business context.

A classic example is the short-sighted career decision, which we'll call 'The Case of the Greener Pastures'.

Case study: Greener Pastures _____

Careers, like businesses, product lines and people, seem to be a constant source of both satisfactions and problems. On the problems side, one of the most common phenomena is the lure of the greener pastures which spread out lushly before us, just on the other side of the fence.

'I wasn't dreadfully unhappy. I've got to say that right at the outset. I had done well in a straight selling role at Mars and I moved quickly into sales management. And as a training ground, it was probably the best company

that anyone could ever work for. But we were mortgaged up to the hilt and we had a second child on the way and, at the same time and because of the quick strides I had made, I was probably getting a bit of an exaggerated sense of my own worth on the market. I can remember joking about the fact that, if footballers could move around from club to club every couple of years and end up earning £50,000 a week and driving a Porsche, then why shouldn't I be doing the same sort of thing.'

The 'problem' came in the form of a rather flattering job offer that, if not actually impossible to turn down, was at least difficult to ignore altogether.

'I had lunch with a headhunter who had somehow got my name and seemed to know all about what I had done at Mars. And I must say I felt rather flattered by the whole situation. To make a long story short, I ended up moving to a small company that was importing and distributing breads and biscuits and pastas from Italy. I liked the people who were running the business and the whole thing had an entrepreneurial flavour to it that was really exciting. Plus, it gave me a chance to really challenge myself and make my mark. My lofty title was Director of Sales and Marketing, there was a rather nice company car involved – a BMW, and the financial package was as they say, too good to turn down. So away I went.'

That was three years ago, and it was an ill-advised move.

'A year-and-a-half into the job, I knew I had made a mistake. In fact, I knew it within months. Sure, the money and the title were there, but I was effectively working – and working awfully damned hard – as a glorified sales rep, calling on the independents and the regional chains and hustling to get our product in there. Meanwhile, the whole industry was changing in some very dramatic and exciting ways, with the multiples taking a bigger and bigger share of the pie and getting themselves involved in everything from banking to selling computers. And I was missing out.'

Remember that we've defined a 'problem' as a gap between the way things are and the way we would want them to be. We've just described the first half of the gap. Here's the second:

'What I really wanted to do was call on Tesco. Or Sainsbury's. Or Safeways. I wanted to be back in the big leagues, doing business on a large scale, working with the big national accounts. If you're in consumer products, then

that's where the excitement is. That's where the growth is. That's where you get involved with the companies and the people who are driving the whole industry. And if you're good at what you do, that's where you want to compete.' _____

Summary

In this chapter we looked at choosing the best solution.

- We're at a stage now where a decision has to be made. We've laid out a series of solution options. Our goal is to choose the best one.
- Best in terms of its impact on the real world.
- *Get the process right.* That is a *mantra* that we should be repeating to ourselves over and over again until we get sick of hearing it.
- Decisions should always be tested out before we commit to them.
- Few things are more conducive to straight thinking than talking a decision through with someone, or writing it out on paper.
- Get the right people involved – those whose commitment will drive the process. Decide where and how they should be brought in.
- In evaluating a solution, look at everything that can go wrong. Assess the risks and make sure you are prepared to cover them.
- Get the timing right. In a fast-moving world, the whole problem-solving cycle has to be more sensitive to what is happening.
- Don't allow a one-off decision to harden into rules unless you do it *consciously.*
- Good decisions will often involve a blend of logic and intuition. Both are important, and which we rely on more is a matter of preference.
- When a decision has to be made, make it. Don't wait until 'all the facts are in'. Don't waste time looking for the *perfect* solution.

CHAPTER 8

Implementing the Solution

A problem isn't solved until our decision is translated into effective action, the results monitored, and the problem situation re-assessed.

We have one final step to take, and that is to translate the decision into an effective plan of action – and execute it.

It has to be a detailed plan.

Some planned questions

These are just a few of the questions we have to ask when a proposed solution involves – as most do – more than just one step or one person.

- ◆ What, specifically, is the goal of the proposed action? How will we know when it has been achieved?
- ◆ What action steps are involved in taking us from where we are now to where we want to get to?
- ◆ What's the schedule?
- ◆ Who is responsible for monitoring and expediting those tasks or steps?
- ◆ Who has to be involved at each step along the way?
- ◆ What resources will be needed?
- ◆ What things have to be learned or researched?
- ◆ What costs will be involved? What happens if we go over budget?
- ◆ Do we need a steering committee?
- ◆ Who's in charge?
- ◆ Rumour has it that John voted *against* the proposal. Should we make an effort to turn him around?
- ◆ Is everyone on board? Does everyone know exactly what we are trying to achieve – and why?

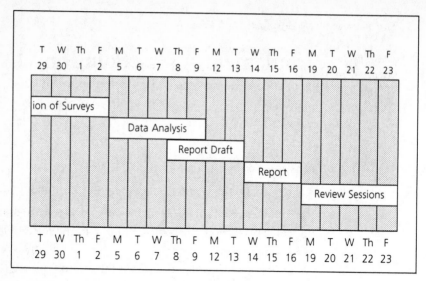

Fig. 23. Visual plan.

Building a visual plan

Unless the actions we propose to take are very simple and few in number, we would be wise to develop some sort of visual overview of our total action plan. A visual representation helps us reason through the sequence of events and helps us spot potential conflicts amongst the steps involved.

At times, a simple schedule of events will do. At other times, we'll need a proper flow chart that shows how the various steps will link up and overlap. In either case, let's remember that the representation is a means to an end, the end being clarity of thinking and effectiveness of control, rather than an end in itself.

A *visual plan* (Figure 23) seems to work well with solutions which involve more than just a simple series of action steps. It breaks the total solution into a series of major action *chunks* and plots them on a planning calendar so that they can be seen at a glance.

1. Define the objective

We have to make sure that we are very clear about our objective. We are talking here about the end result that the solution as a whole – we'll refer to it as a 'project' – has to accomplish, and the date by which that has to be done.

2. *Identify the major chunks*

Next, we break the project as a whole down into its major component parts. Each part should be a *chunk* of activity with an identifiable beginning and end and the parts, when strung together end to end, should add up to the successful completion of the project as a whole.

4. *Define a goal for each chunk*

It is useful to articulate the *Goal* for each of the major chunks identified in Step 2.

The goals ought to be *major* goals. And that will normally mean that something is finalised or produced and, in most cases, delivered to a customer. We define a *customer* as someone who is waiting for an output; it might be an 'external' customer, but it might just as easily be someone down the hall or a department up on the next floor.

4. *Attach a target date to each*

Once our goals have been defined, we attach a target date to each so that the project as a whole will come to a successful completion on time.

5. *Develop an action plan for each goal*

On a separate form or sheet of paper like the one shown in Figure 24, each goal can then be broken down into its component action steps, with each step being assigned its own specific target date. These will guide our day-to-day, hour-by-hour activities.

The art of delegation

We generally think of delegation as being something that *managers* do. But that needn't be the case.

Later on in the book – Chapter 13 – we will be turning our attention to you as a manager as distinct from you as an individual problem-solver. At this stage, however, we're going to look at delegation as part of what's needed to bring a project to a

Action Plan		
Label:		
Goal:		
	Action	Deadline
1		
2		
3		
4		
5		
6		
7		
8		

Fig. 24. Action plan.

successful conclusion. It's part of any solution which involves more work than a single person can handle.

And, of course, it's also part of managing in the more traditional sense. As a manager, you can best *maximise* your value to your employer by *developing* and *identifying* solutions – not *implementing* them. The art of being a successful manager rests heavily on the principle of *leverage*. Exercising leverage means multiplying your impact. Making a decision that affects how ten different people will go about their jobs is a high-leverage activity. Telling Joe what to do about the problem with the store manager in Leeds is a low-leverage activity. By and large, there are two classes of activity in which you – as a manager – should be engaged:

- Things which have a widespread impact extending beyond your own personal work.
- Things which require your unique managerial perspective, experience, insight, status, or clout.

There is a second factor, of course. Decisions about what to do are best taken by those closest to the scene of the action. Factory problems are best solved by people on the factory floor. The closer we get to the scene of the action, the more specific and up-to-date is the information on which the problem-solving will be based.

For our purposes, there are probably three key rules that we need to follow (Figure 25). Let's go through them one by one.

1. Delegate by results

This is perhaps the most important principle of effective delegation – don't give people tasks to do, give them a result to achieve. Don't look over their shoulders. Give them room to think for themselves. Agree on what results have to be accomplished and then let them go to it:

- Make sure that the objective, and the date by which it has to be achieved, are absolutely clear.
- Spell out the ground rules – when you should be consulted, when initiative is to be exercised, and so on.
- Take time at the outset to give the other person your 'feel' for the problem.
- Ask the individual to prepare a plan of action showing how expected results will be accomplished.
- Make sure that the person has the authority needed to carry out all parts of the delegated assignment.

And then – don't interfere. From that point on, the other person carries the ball. Easy to say but difficult to make it stick. Too many managers delegate in theory, but then start meddling – asking about the fine details, offering 'suggestions' in a way which clearly pressures the other person into acting on them, and so on. Nothing communicates more clearly the fact that we don't really have confidence in the employee's capacity to decide what has to be done.

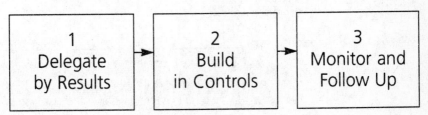

Fig. 25. Three key rules.

2. Build in controls

When we pass work down to someone on our team, we have to discipline ourselves to let the person take the ball and run with it – but we also need to exercise our ultimate responsibility for the work that is done. And the logical way to balance these two needs is to build in a system of checkpoints and controls. So what we do is agree on a way of keeping in touch right from the outset:

- Build in controls – action plans, deadlines, periodic progress reports, and so on.
- Arrange informal interim meetings for periodic discussion and evaluation of progress.
- Follow up on specific tasks to make sure that they have been done properly.
- Keep yourself available to lend assistance if required. Be prepared to step in if necessary.
- But – always – judge by *results*. Don't insist that people do things the way you would do them.

3. Monitor and follow up

Jennifer Adair, one of our *Famous Five*, uses the Quality Assurance principle of *spot-checking* to develop a sense of how a delegated project is being carried out.

Case study: Jennifer Adair _____

'When I've delegated something, I do spot-checks on how the person is doing. I pick one or two specific aspects of the project and ask some very explicit questions that require a fairly detailed response. That allows me to really get a sense of whether the person is on top of things. If his or her answer is convincing, then I can rest easy and assume that the project as a whole is in good hands and coming along nicely.' _____

On the subject of delegation, another of our *Famous Five*, Jack Carter, had this advice:

Case study: Jack Carter _____

'If you're going to check something, check it early on in the process. Review a rough draft of a report, for example, rather than waiting until the other person has spent a lot of time putting it into final form and polishing off all the rough edges. That way, there's less re-work needed. Try to approve what

the person plans to do, and the thinking behind that plan, rather than the
execution.' _____

A point worth noting – as the comments of both Jennifer and Jack
would imply, monitoring and following up isn't meddling. It's
part and parcel of managing. It's the logical, essential, and
perfectly legitimate other side of the delegation coin.

Maximising your chances

When you put forth a proposed solution to a problem you are
usually competing for scarce resources. Other people have their
own problems to solve and are putting forward their own ideas
about what should be done. Not everything can be acted upon.
Constraints in terms of time and money and equipment and
people mean that choices have to be made.

And you want those choices to be made in favour of *your*
solution. Here are just a few guidelines to help ensure that your
needs are given the consideration they deserve.

Focus on today's priorities, not yesterday's

> You should make sure that what was a high priority two months
> ago is still a high priority ...

If you were given a golden opportunity to solve a problem two
months ago and are just now getting ready to present your
strategy to the powers that be, you should make sure that what
was a high priority two months ago is still a high priority.

It is absolutely astounding how quickly things change in today's
business environment. When someone hands us an invitation to
take an in-depth look at a high-priority issue it is imperative
that we take a look, almost *daily*, to make sure that the issue
hasn't shifted in some subtle way and that its priority hasn't
changed.

Get the key people involved

We've talked about the involvement of other people before, and
we will probably talk about it again. Anyone whose enthusiastic

and diligent execution is crucial to success should be involved as early on and as extensively as possible.

And that will apply to most of the problem-solving we do. There aren't too many problems worth solving that don't have an impact on other people. Not these days. And there aren't too many solutions that don't need to be executed and managed through a total team effort.

Polish your presentation skills

> Don't spoil a good proposal by presenting it in lack-lustre fashion to the group whose go-ahead or backing is vital to its success.

Some people seem to have been born with the ability to get up and dazzle an audience. For most of us, however, our manner of presenting an idea or proposal will tend to *detract* from its impact rather than *adding* to it ... *unless* we take specific steps to develop our presentation skills. The ability to give a positive presentation, in other words, is something that has to be *learned*.

Thankfully, there is plenty of help around. There is almost no end to the number of training courses and seminars that have to do with presentation skills. There is also a wide array of audio tapes, videos, and books available for the person who wants to do his or her self-development work at home.

More than confidence and polish and flair, what makes a presentation successful is some disciplined attention – beforehand – to some very practical tasks:

- Find out who exactly will be at the meeting and what role they play in the decision-making process.
- Write down your goal for the meeting – what you want to come away with or what specific *actions* you want people to take.
- Write down what each of the people on the *other* side of the table will want to come away with.
- Think through the key concepts which you will need to implant in the audience's mind. What has to *change* inside their heads?
- Think through and prepare for the queries, or challenges you might need to deal with. Don't be caught by surprise.

- ◆ Think through people's current perceptions or feelings about the issues that will be discussed.
- ◆ Identify what they will need to see in order to commit themselves to the action that will be recommended.
- ◆ Identify the 'style' of communication that will best allow these ends to be achieved.

Making things happen

We talked in an earlier chapter about putting together an employee newsletter and we used the newsletter as an example of a *Do-It* problem.

Case study: Jennifer Adair

The example was suggested by Jennifer Adair, one of our *Famous Five*, and she had this to say about how the whole project was managed:

'I'd have to say, at this point, that the whole project has really sputtered and come to a standstill. The original idea of doing a newsletter was certainly well received, and Clare did a nice job of putting together a mock-up and using it to get people's input. But then the whole project seemed to peter out. I think the problem is that no one has really been driving the process. It should be Clare, obviously, but for whatever reason she hasn't really taken charge of things – and if there's one thing I've learned about the way things work around here, it's that things don't happen unless someone makes them happen.'

Things don't happen unless someone makes them happen. That statement probably represents the rule rather than the exception.

Someone has to *drive* the process, *champion* the idea, *spearhead* the change, *expedite* the activity, and generally be the one who *makes things happen*.

If it's your problem, if it's your solution, then you're it. You're the one who has to make things happen.

Assessing results

> We are effectively returning to the problem *awareness* step and seeing whether we need to re-cycle the entire six-step problem-solving process.

Has the solution done its job? Has the problem been solved?

These are the questions we have to ask ourselves at this last stage in the whole problem-solving process. And by asking them we are effectively returning to the problem *awareness* step and seeing whether we need to re-cycle the entire six-step problem-solving process. We've closed the loop. The only question now is whether we still have a problem left to solve. If we do, we go on to Step Two again. If we don't, then we call the whole process to a halt and jot a little reminder in our calendar to look at things again in a week's time.

Learning from our solutions

In hindsight, did we solve the problem in the most efficient and effective way possible? Did we use our time, and the resources around us, to best advantage? Did we base our problem-solving deliberations on the latest and most complete information? Did we consider a full range of possible solutions before deciding which one to move ahead with?

It is well worth asking these questions, and taking time to answer them properly.

Case study: Jack Carter ————————————————————
Jack Carter again:

> *'One of the things that really impresses me about top performers is that they are always questioning themselves and scrutinising their own performance. It's probably the single most consistent thing that sets them apart from average people. They actually take time to sit down and think about themselves. And they want feedback; they'll lap up whatever feedback you can give them.'* ————————————————————

Problem-solving, like any other competency or skill, is something we *should* get better at as we go along. And that happens to the extent that we spend a bit of time scrutinising our own performance and tracking down specific areas where a bit of fine-tuning might be in order.

Summary

In this chapter we looked at planning, implementing and evaluating our actions.

- Good execution starts with planning. Work through the details. If something goes wrong, it will almost always be because of a *detail*.
- It is a good idea to build a *visual plan* if the solution involves several people or several steps.
- Get the right people involved – people whose commitment will drive the process.
- Never under-estimate the ease with which good ideas get neglected because of lack of commitment.
- The presentation of your proposal is often the key to its success.
- Delegation will be part of any solution large enough to require a team effort.
- Successful delegation means attending to three basic rules: (1) delegate by results, (2) build in controls, and (3) monitor and follow up.
- Things don't happen unless you make them happen.
- The problem-solving cycle isn't complete until we have assessed results and re-started the cycle if necessary.

CHAPTER 9

Creativity

T he ability to 'come up with something' when something is needed … that's what we're going to work on in this chapter.

Last year, because I was laid up in hospital for ten days following a serious operation, and because I wasn't in any shape to do any physical labour for two or three months thereafter, the grass in our back lawn grew to a point where it was virtually impossible to cut. It was also soggy, because it had rained almost every single day during June.

Someone beat me to it

To cut a long story short, I eventually cut the whole lawn using a strimmer – and I burnt out the strimmer's motor in the process. Then I still had to go through the whole process again using the lawn mower.

Ah hah! What the world needs, I thought to myself, is a combination strimmer-lawn-mower that can do both jobs at once. Lo and behold, I looked in a newspaper recently and saw not one but *two* advertisements for combination lawn-mowers and strimmers which are exactly like what I had in mind.

Think of the money I could have made.

Ah well. Let's think creatively on those occasions when something new and different is needed to bridge the gap between the way things are and the way they ought to be.

Two forms

In practice, creativity seems to come in two main forms:

♦ In a situation where there is no routine or standard solution to the problem the creative person comes up with an effective response.

♦ In a situation where there *is* a routine or standard solution the creative person comes up with something *new and better.*

The creative person will look for something that's new and different. This is creativity not so much in the traditional problem-*solving* sense, but more in the context of problem *creating.* If it ain't broke, in other words, *break it.*

Analytical barriers to creativity

The first step in tapping our creative ability is to clear away the 'blinders' which tend to inhibit creativity. Here are two of the most common culprits:

♦ *Overreliance on logic and precision:* It starts at school. We learn to equate logical or inductive reasoning with 'thinking' in general.

♦ *Black-and-white thinking.* The human brain has a neat way of simplifying things if we allow it to. It eases 'cognitive strain' by translating things into black and white whenever it can.

Emotional barriers to creativity

Emotional habits and hang-ups can dampen creativity. Here are two of the most common examples:

♦ *Fear of ridicule:* Stick with the tried and true. Keep your wild ideas to yourself. Unless you're prepared to go out on a limb then you're not going to be very creative.

♦ *Failure to aim high:* Settling for a satisfactory result rather than aiming for an optimal outcome. An adequate solution can generally be borrowed from what we did last week or last month. An *optimal* solution, on the other hand, will have to be invented.

Ten ways to become more creative

We're struggling to solve a problem. There's no standard or routine or prescribed response that we can fall back on. So we're going to have to *come up with something.*

1. *Visualise the end result*

If you listen to the *Andante* of the Piano Concerto No. 21 in C it is difficult to believe that music of such sublime beauty was actually composed by a human being. Indeed, it is instructive to hear what Mozart himself had to say about the process:

> 'First bits and crumbs of the piece come and gradually join together in my mind; then the soul getting warmed to the work, the thing grows more and more, and I spread it out broader and clearer, and at least it gets almost finished in my head, even when it is a long piece, so that I can see the whole of it at a single glance in my mind, as if it were a beautiful painting or a handsome human being.'

This is a good example of someone *imagining* the end result in their mind's eye before it has actually been created. It has been said that Michaelangelo, asked how he created the statue of David, said '*I started with a huge block of stone and simply chipped away all the parts that weren't David*'. The idea here is the same, and the capacity to *visualise* the end result seems to play some sort of central role in the creative process.

Can we *train* ourselves to it – to visualise the end result? Yes we can, to a much greater extent than we realise. How? By *doing it*. Just doing it – and getting better with practice. Wrestling with a thorny problem? Unable to decide what to do? Try this:

> *Sit back. Relax. Close your eyes. Loosen your shoulders. Take a deep breath, and let it out slowly. Now ... imagine yourself having solved the problem. Develop the scene in your mind, as if you were watching it on video. You're relaxed; the tension is gone; the problem has been solved; the solution works; you're happy with it.*

Not all problems will lend themselves to this sort of approach. But many can. Even something as seemingly mundane as ...

> '*I was getting myself into a real stew, knowing that all these people from Jack's office were going to be coming to our house on Saturday evening. I worried about seating arrangements, and*

*whether we should have Justin open his gifts before or after the
meal, and what sort of music I should put on, and whether I
should get Jack to have someone bring a video camera along …'*

Sound familiar?

*'And then I sat down, and relaxed, and tried to visualise the best
and most enjoyable evening these people had had for a long time.
And what I saw was people relaxing, enjoying themselves, not
being squeezed into a schedule or being paraded from this room
into that room. What struck me was the spontaneity of the whole
thing, the casual ease with which people decided who they
wanted to talk to or where they wanted to sit. So I decided to
relax, curb my natural inclination to want to over-manage
everything, and just let the universe unfold in its own merry way.'*

2. Think backwards

> We start with the end result – and then work backwards to see
> how we got there.

This is very similar to visualising the end result but then we go a
step further. We start with the end result – and then work
backwards to see how we got there. Watch it unfold in your
mind's eye as if you were watching a video recording.

Our problem is to reduce turnover on the sales team. Pay them
more money? That's one solution that we will undoubtedly want
to look at, because we know for a fact that two or three of our top
people have left because they could earn a good £10,000 more
with a competitor. It's the *logical* solution.

But let's simply close our eyes and develop a mental image of
how things might be once our problem has been solved.

*It's a year from now. Our turnover rate is not hitting us where it
hurts. Most of the people who leave are people we can afford to
lose, or who shouldn't have been here in the first place. Our top
people are happy, and that's the main thing. Why are they happy?
Because they are treated like senior professionals. They are
earning good money. They are being challenged to develop their*

business and management skills. They are developing their teamwork and decision-making skills. They are being given a chance to really come up with innovative ideas that they can take to their customers. Leave? No, they wouldn't dream of it. Whether their long-term goal is to move into a Director of Sales and Marketing slot or be a consultant or run their own business, there's no better training ground in the world than what they have right now.

There's nothing magic here. We're simply describing a future state of affairs as if it existed right now.

And we're doing it in a spontaneous fashion. That is very important. It's a bit like 'brainstorming', except what we're doing here is describing a state of affairs in our mind's eye. In effect, we're inventing the future.

Now ... what did we do or say, or what happened, that led to that state of affairs?

3. Talk it through

> Talking something through forces us to be clear-headed.

You're talking with Jack.

You: *Once we've got an agreement, the plan is that we then take the whole issue to the Directors and hopefully get them to release the funds.*

Jack: *Why take it up to the Director level?*

You: *Well, at some stage we have to get their approval. That seems pretty obvious.*

Jack: *What I mean is, why not do it earlier? Why not get them involved at an earlier stage?*

If the essence of creativity is the ability to come at something from a whole new angle, then it makes sense to assume that Jack is more apt to do that than *you* are. That's because they will come at it with an uncluttered mind. You won't.

And they can only do that if you talk to them. If you take time to bounce your ideas off them and get their reaction.

The other thing about talking something through, of course, is that it *forces* us to be clear-headed.

4. Go for a long walk

Actually get out of the building. Go and spend some time with the pigeons and the squirrels.

Divide your walk into two parts. During the first part, concentrate on deep breathing. Breathing from the diaphragm. In, out, in, out. Deep breaths that send air right down into the middle of your body. If thoughts come into your mind, don't dwell on them or do anything with them. Just let them drift away. Focus on the breathing.

During the second part of your walk, shift your focus to the problem you've been wrestling with. You might want to sit down on a park bench while you do this, or gaze out onto the water.

Pigeons, squirrels, park benches, water ... give your brain some breathing space. They give your whole body an opportunity to 'wind down'.

It's the release of tension that is the secret. Tension and creativity are like chalk and cheese. To get your creative juices flowing, you need to get yourself into a relaxed frame of mind.

> Pigeons, squirrels, park benches, water ... give your brain some breathing space.

5. Draw a picture of the problem

Sketch it out using boxes and circles and arrows. Use words as labels where appropriate but try not to write any elaborate *text*. Stick to pictures.

Drawing a picture is a very important aid to creativity for a number of reasons:

◆ It allows the interconnections between events or items to be shown visually.

◆ Visual representation allows a great deal of information and ideas to be captured on a single page where we can see it at a glance.

◆ It *cuts down* on the amount of information we need. A few boxes and arrows accompanied by some brief labels or notes can replace *pages and pages* of linear text.

◆ We can keep related ideas and facts together.

6. *Play around with ideas*

Play with them. Turn them over in your mind. Sleep on them. Talk about them over lunch with a friend or colleague. Tell your dog about them.

There's an element of *playfulness* here, and most studies of creative people have reported that this *playfulness* is a consistent part of what distinguishes the creative thinker from his or her colleagues.

- I wonder what would happen if ...?
- Wouldn't it be fun to try ...?
- Has anyone ever tried ...?
- I know this sounds far-out, but could we try ...?

These are the sorts of exploratory, speculative statements which encourage us to think *outside the box.*

7. *Think positively*

One of the reasons some people don't spend enough time *toying* with ideas is that they are too quick to reject an unusual idea as not worth toying with.

Even if an idea seems far-fetched, don't dismiss it out of hand. Try to appreciate its good points, and look for something to *build* upon.

That's the sort of attitude – an open-mindedness, a fundamental *positiveness* – that encourages people to come forward with ideas.

8. *Sleep on it*

As a last resort, put the whole thing aside and come back to it tomorrow. Worrying about it isn't going to do any good.

And *not* worrying about it *will.* Putting something aside and coming back to it the next day is one of those 'techniques' that you'll find described in every book on creative thinking that has ever been written.

The technique is generally called *incubation,* and it is generally assumed that – once the facts and information available to us have been properly gathered, organised, and analysed – our subconscious needs a chance to 'chew' on things and point us in the right direction.

It doesn't always work but sleeping is a lot more restful and enjoyable than banging your head against a brick wall. Even if all it does is allow you to come back to the very same point the next day with an invigorated spirit then 'good sleep' is a problem-solving tool that none of us should go without.

9. Do a lot of reading

Both successful executives and creative thinkers tend to be voracious readers. They display a thirst for knowledge that draws them not only to books but to the world of arts, to stimulating companions and discussion, to exotic travel destinations, and to the serious pursuit of enriching hobbies.

Case study: Tony Martindale _____

The debonair and well-read Tony Martindale, one of our *Famous Five*, had this to say:

> '*I remember being told that studying Latin was good for people because it was a way of exercising the brain, in much the same way that we exercise other parts of our body. At some level, I suppose I've never quite left that belief behind. The reason I enjoy a good game of chess, or a trip to the Tate Gallery, is because it activates and expands and challenges my mind. In some way or another, and it's not crucial that I know exactly how this happens, it makes my mind stronger.*' _____

Successful executives and creative thinkers are able to draw upon a storehouse of knowledge in ways which the more pedestrian thinker is unable to match. A chess strategy becomes the inspiration for a bold initiative in the marketplace. A painting at the Tate Gallery is used to illustrate the type of synergistic teamwork that a senior manager is looking for in his or her people.

10. Give the problem to someone creative

It's always good to have at least one friend or colleague who has a distinctly 'creative' way of looking at things. They may not dress right. They don't always show up for work or leave for home at the same time that the rest of us do. And they sometimes say things in meetings that seem childish, naive, even downright *daft* at times. But they *are* creative. They have a different way of looking at things. They come at things from a different angle.

Five ways to encourage creativity in others

One of the real hallmarks of a successful manager is his or her ability to draw out creative thinking and problem-solving from other people.

1. Ask a question

A question that really causes people to have to *think* about what they are doing.

What would happen, Bob, if we simply ignored the Marketing committee altogether and went out and got the samples made ourselves?

How is Kate Larimer going to react to this? If I'm Kate, and I've just read through this summary and seen the data, how am I feeling? What's my gut reaction?

What we are doing here is getting people to look at things from another perspective. And the asking of *questions* is the most obvious route to generating multiple perspectives.

2. Listen

> If rule number one is to ask a question, then rule number two is to listen carefully to the answer.

Let the other person talk. Don't interrupt. Focus on understanding and fully *appreciating* what the person is saying.

The only time we need to say anything is when a word of encouragement is needed to get the person to expand upon a thought or develop it further. Often, all that's needed is a slight nod of the head – anything that says that we're mentally *working* on what we have heard, and would like to   hear more.

3. Acknowledge an idea's merit

The key thing is to be open-minded and non-judgmental. In fact, let's go a step further and be downright *positive*. Even if the idea is far-fetched we should still praise the person for putting it forward and look for something to build upon. What we *shouldn't* do is dismiss it out of hand.

Ummm, that's an interesting idea, Frances. I'm not sure the committee would buy it, but if we could somehow shift the emphasis a bit from …

4. Don't focus on the details

When someone puts an idea forward, don't pick away at the details. There will be a time and a place for examining them. Focus instead on the *gist* of the idea, on the essential *thrust* of the proposal. The details can be dealt with later.

5. Show enthusiasm

This is very a simple way in which a manager can add value to the problem-solving process. By expressing enthusiasm for an idea.

That sounds great, Bill! – a simple comment like that, voiced with enthusiasm, will mean much more to Bill than you can possibly imagine. Your enthusiastic reception will allow him to relax, get into the swing of things, unleash his own enthusiasm, and – most importantly – get his mental juices flowing.

Summary

In this chapter we have looked at the importance of creativity in the problem-solving process.

- In a situation where there is no routine or standard solution to the problem, the creative person comes up with an effective response.
- In a situation where there *is* a routine or standard solution to the problem, the creative person comes up with something *new and better*.
- The capacity to *visualise* the end result plays a central role in the creative process.
- We can visualise the end result – and then work backwards to see how we got there.

- Talking to people is one of the most useful things we can do. It forces us to be clear-headed.
- Plus, other people are more likely than we are to come at a problem with an uncluttered mind.
- Go and spend some time with the pigeons and the squirrels.
- Tension and creativity are like chalk and cheese. You need to get yourself into a relaxed frame of mind.
- Play around with ideas. Sleep on them. Tell your dog about them.
- Even if an idea seems far-fetched, don't dismiss it out of hand. Look for something to build upon.

CHAPTER 10

Intuition

O ur 'little Black Box' – and yes, each of us has one – has a very important role to play in the problem-solving process.

We took our first look at Intuition – as part of *Choosing the Best Solution* – back in chapter 7. In this chapter, we're going to take a more detailed look … and our goal will be not just to understand intuitive thinking but to put it to fruitful use at all stages in the problem-solving cycle.

First, some facts. Successful managers rely a great deal on intuitive thinking as a problem-solving tool. They do so not as an *alternative* to a more systematic or logical approach but as a complement to it.

Intuition at Work

In the Christmas 1984 edition of the *Harvard Business Review* Daniel Isenberg reported on two years of observational work with a dozen senior American managers – all responsible for the performance of their respective business units.

> 'They seldom think in ways that one might simplistically view as "rational"; i.e., they rarely systematically formulate goals, assess their worth, evaluate the probabilities of alternative ways of reaching them, and choose the path that maximises expected return. Rather, managers frequently bypass rigorous, analytical planning altogether, particularly when they face difficult, novel, or extremely entangled decisions. When they do use analysis for a prolonged time, it is always in conjunction with intuition.'

Intuition seems to enter into the manager's day-to-day problem-solving activity in a number of ways:

◆ Intuition allows a manager to sense when a problem exists or is about to emerge. Something isn't right. Something doesn't fit. They can sense it.

◆ Intuition is what allows a manager to perform a routine task – something he/she has done a hundred times before – quickly and without thinking. They seem to be able to do it almost automatically – the way a professional photographer quickly adjusts the focus ring, aperture, and speed dial of the camera without taking his or her eye off the subject.

◆ It is quite common for managers to use intuition as a check on the results of a more systematic or rational analysis. The data is in and the manager asks *Does all this match what my gut feel has been telling me? Does it look right and feel right?*

Back to Daniel Isenberg:

'By now it should be clear that intuition is not the opposite of rationality, nor is it a random process of guessing. Rather, it is based on extensive experience both in analysis and problem solving and in implementation, and to the extent that the lessons of experience are logical and well-founded, then so is the intuition. Further, managers often combine gut feel with systematic analysis, quantified data, and thoughtfulness.

It should also be clear that executives use intuition during all phases of the problem-solving process: problem finding, problem defining, generating and choosing a solution, and implementing the solution. In fact, senior managers often ignore the implied linear progression of the rational decision-making model and jump opportunistically from phase to phase, allowing implementation concerns to affect the problem definition and perhaps even to limit the range of solutions generated.'

Isenberg also studied how top executives make decisions. His conclusions confirmed that executives do indeed rely very heavily on intuition as a problem-solving and decision-making tool.

'The executives were quick to point out that they considered intuition to be only one tool of many to use in guiding their decisions. They did not advocate relying exclusively on intuition or abandoning traditional "left-brain" management practices. On the other hand, respondents emphasised that intuition is also a key

management resource that should be used to help guide strategic decisions.'

Understanding intuition

It should be clear that intuition, rather than being an alternative to a more disciplined or rigorous mode of thinking, is actually a complement to it. The two work together as allies.

When a radiologist says 'I have a feeling that it's this little blob here, this dark spot, that's causing all the problems', or when a lawnmower dealer tells you 'My hunch is that this machine isn't worth fixing', what we're getting is an intuitive judgement or prediction based on literally *years* of studied practise. Over the years, the person has worked systematically through enough problems to be in a position now to *sense* what's happening or about to happen.

Researchers have established that information in long-term memory is sorted into clusters. When we face a new problem our mind performs a 'search' through this stored information to see if it can find a similar or relevant experience. If it does we get a 'flash' of insight, experienced as intuition.

This is Lord Thomson, in his autobiography *After I Was Sixty*, talking about his moving to London at a time – in his late 60's – when most other people have retired:

> 'At various times during my business life I have had to take some important decisions and, particularly in the early days, I often got these wrong. But I found later that the early mistakes and, for that matter, the early correct decisions stood me in good stead. Most of the problems that I was confronted with in London were in one way or another related to those earlier ones. It was often a matter of just adding some zeros to figures and the sums were the same. In a great many instances I knew the answer immediately. I cannot explain this scientifically, but I was entirely convinced that, through the years, in my brain as in a computer, I had stored details of the problems themselves, the decisions reached, and the results obtained. Everything was neatly filed away there for future use. Then, later, when a new problem arose, I would think it over and, if the answer was not immediately apparent, I would let it go for a while, and it was as if it went the rounds of

the brain cells looking for guidance that could be retrieved, for by the next morning, when I examined the problem again, more often than not the solution came up right away. That judgement seemed to come almost subconsciously, and my conviction is that during the time I was not consciously considering the problem, my subconscious had been turning it over and relating it to my memory; it had been held up to the light of the experiences I have had in past years, and the way through the difficulties became obvious.'

The idea that our brain stores information about its successes and failures and then uses it to generate solutions to problems is certainly not far-fetched. Most of us have had 'ah-hah' experiences where the answer to a problem has spontaneously come into our mind.

When intuition is helpful

In management circles, intuition has become an increasingly *valued* commodity. True, managers are still trained and evaluated along rational lines but intuition is no longer seen as something *alien* that has to be excluded from the manager's intellectual tool kit.

Here are just a few of the situations where it becomes a well-nigh *essential* part of the problem-solving process:

◆ Hard facts are few and far between, but the situation demands a decision regardless.
◆ The facts are there, but they don't point the way clearly; they don't tell us what to do.
◆ Time is a factor. Extensive fact-gathering and analysis simply isn't going to be possible.
◆ There are several feasible solutions, all logically defensible. A judgement call is required.

Note that these are all *decision-making* situations, reflecting the fact that intuition comes into play most significantly in the decision-making stages of the problem-solving cycle.

But intuition also plays an important part at other stages in the cycle. At the initial *Awareness* stage effective managers use their intuitive powers to sniff out potential problems before they emerge full-blown. During the *Information* and *Definition* stages of the cycle, their intuition allows them to develop a *feel* for how people are reacting to an event and to develop a cognitive *map* of the situation that they are dealing with.

So intuition is a well-nigh essential problem-solving tool without which a manager isn't likely to be optimally effective.

And that raises the question. Can intuition be *developed*?

Everyday intuition

Most of us rely quite heavily on intuition when we choose a new dress or a new suit.

Taking a little bit of evidence – an early warning signal – and filling in the gaps ... it's something that all of us do in everyday situations. Some of us can *sense* when a car needs a good service, we don't need to hear something clanging under the bonnet.

So when our daughter announces 'Something tells me that Peter isn't feeling very well' – Peter being her pet rabbit – it is futile to respond with a logical question (*What makes you say that?*). We simply have to acknowledge that she probably knows what she's talking about.

But how does it actually work?

Most of us rely quite heavily on intuition when we choose a new dress or a new suit. We're after a red dress that we can wear to the party on Saturday, or a dark blue suit to replace the one with the frayed cuffs.

Beyond that, however, most of us will try on a series of dresses or suits until we find one that we like. We look at ourselves in the mirror. We look, in effect, *holistically* – at the whole person. We make a judgement call and slot the dress or suit into one of two categories:

- *That's me!*
- *That's just not me.*

This is what seems to be happening:

- We look at the situation *visually* – not logically. We actually *look* rather than *analyse* or *think*.
- We look at it holistically. We look at ourselves, in the new dress or suit, in a full-length mirror.

- We develop an overall sense of whether there's a good fit or a bad fit, a 'right' or a 'wrong'.

Developing intuition

Intuition, then, isn't something that only a minority of people have access to. It is something that all of us use and experience in a wide range of everyday situations. Can we learn to apply this same process to work-related situations and problems? That's the question.

1. Relax the thinking process

To allow intuitive data to come to the surface, you have to turn off the conscious 'thinking' part of your brain. Or leave it on but change stations.

Do something else. Take a break. Put the problem away and turn your attention to something altogether different.

We talked about this in relation to creativity. If you're at the office, put your coat on and go for a walk. Go and spend some time with the pigeons and the squirrels …

2. Listen to your inner voice

Each of us has a little voice inside us. It makes its presence felt in a variety of ways.

I can't bring myself to toss an empty pop can out the window of my car. If I did it accidentally I'd have to go back and pick it up. I couldn't just leave it there.

That's one way our little voice acts as a 'conscience'. It tells us whether we've done good or bad. It steers us away from doing things that are inconsistent with our 'values' or 'beliefs'.

At other times, intuition takes the form of a *leaning* – that's the way it feels … we're *leaning* toward a specific option in a decision-making situation:

My gut feel says 'Go with it'. I think if we wait until all the data is in, we'll still be faced with the need to make a judgement. And my instincts are telling me that if we don't move now, we're going to end up missing one hell of an opportunity.

At other times, it's not so much a leaning as it is a warning signal, a red flag, a vague feeling of discomfort:

My instincts are telling me that we should just stop this whole thing right now and go right back to our original mandate.

3. Trust your intuition

Too often, we tell the people around us – after an event has occurred – I had a hunch that would happen! If that was the case, why didn't we speak up *before* the event? Why didn't we *say* something?

Because we were afraid of looking foolish, most likely. Not quite willing to really *trust* intuition.

Or, in some cases, we trusted our intuition but would have been hard-pressed to defend it logically.

You: *Hold on, Linda, that's not going to work, I just know it. We'll end up further in the hole than we are now.*

Linda: *Why's that?*

You: *I don't know … I've just got a gut feel that we're doing this the wrong way …*

Not a very compelling argument, is it?

4. Translate the intuition into action terms

If you announce that your instincts are telling you that such-and-such an option is bad – *I've got a hunch that Susan's group isn't going to be very comfortable with that line of reasoning* – they're going to ask you *why*. In other words, they're going to ask you to translate your intuition into factual, rational terms. It is much better to phrase your intuitive comment so that it refers to an action:

Something tells me that this might be a good place to stop and take a breather.

My feeling is, and it's just a gut feel, that we should move ahead now, while we have the chance.

My instincts are telling me that we're moving too quickly here, that we've overlooked something.

I've got a hunch that, if we approach Jim with this now, we're going to get royally screwed.

The first two statements refer to an action. The second two statements do so in a somewhat more *implicit* fashion. However, the result is the same. It invites people to say either yes or no and then to share their own thoughts about the matter.

Summary

In this chapter we looked at how intuition can be used as a problem-solving tool.

- Studies show that managers use intuition as a problem-solving tool – not as an *alternative* to rationality but as a complement to it.
- Intuition allows a manager to sense when a problem exists or is about to emerge.
- Intuition allows a manager to perform a routine task quickly and without thinking.
- It is quite common for managers to use intuition as a check on the results of a more systematic or rational analysis.
- Our subconscious mind will continue to work on a problem long after we have turned our conscious attention to something else.
- Our brain stores information about its successes and failures and then uses that information to generate solutions to problems.
- Intuition plays an important role throughout the entire problem-solving cycle.
- It is especially useful when facts don't point the way clearly toward a solution, and a judgement call is needed.
- Intuition does not require special training or powers. Most of us rely quite heavily on intuition when we choose a new dress or a new suit.
- The key to *developing* intuition is to relax and *trust* what your inner voice is telling you when it makes its presence felt.

CHAPTER 11

Strategic Thinking

T he capacity to move deftly between the macro and the micro view of things is probably the most crucial skill in our problem-solving toolkit.

Let's acknowledge that there are *other* books on problem-solving that you could be reading.

Leaf through those other books on problem-solving, however, and you won't find a chapter on *Strategic Thinking.* You won't find a chapter on:

- ◆ Dealing with Complexity
- ◆ Dealing with Ambiguity
- ◆ Seeing the Real Issues
- ◆ Seeing the Forest Through the Trees
- ◆ Going to the Heart of the Matter
- ◆ Seeing the Big Picture.

Effective problem-solving

And yet ... most of us will recognise right away that there is something here that gets to the heart of what effective problem-solving is all about.

Jennifer Adair, one of our *Famous Five*, certainly recognises it.

'One of the things I want our customer service people to be doing is thinking strategically and taking a strategic approach to solving customer problems. What that means is thinking about the problem behind the problem – and trying not just to solve the immediate problem at hand but also to address the larger issue which lies behind it.'

Tony Martindale, another of our *Famous Five*, is also aware of the importance of being 'strategic'.

> *'Rather than just moving into action, I think people have to stop and think through what sort of approach – on a more general level – is going to maximise their business results. You can't just go in there and sell, sell, sell anymore. You have to know how you want to position yourself – and that means that you have to understand the things that drive the customer's business.'*

The problem is that it is very difficult to define. No one seems to be quite sure exactly what it is, and that makes it difficult to describe how to *do* it.

So ... let's break some new ground.

A question of strategy

A 'strategy' is an approach to something. It's a way of tackling a problem or working toward an objective.

- What approach should we take?
- How should we come at this?
- How should we be trying to position ourselves?
- What's the best overall way to do this?

These are 'strategic' questions.

A 'strategy' is an *approach* to something. It's a *way* of tackling a problem or working toward an objective. It's a common thread that runs through all the steps we'll be taking and ties them together.

- Our objective is to win the match with Inter Milan. Our *strategy* is to play an *attacking* game that keeps the talented Italian team on its back foot.
- Our objective is to get our line of children's clothes sold through Safeway. Our strategy is to demonstrate to Safeway that we will work with them to attract more customers into their stores.

In all of these cases we are plotting a *general approach* that will guide our more specific actions as we solve our problem. We can play an English-style *kick-and-chase* game or opt for a more

European *skill-and-possession* approach – and we have to choose which way to play.

Let's take a closer look at strategic thinking.

Step 1 – stop and think

> What we have to do, if we're going to think strategically, is shift the focus from action to understanding.

Let's go back to a situation which we first visited in Chapter 5. The problem had to do with lagging sales.

Working behind the scenes on this one was Jack Carter, divisional director and one of our *Famous Five*.

> *'Back in the old days, when sales were falling off a bit, you used to just crack the whip. In effect, you pushed the pressure down the ladder – "Start hustling, you guys … get out there and sell!". This time around, however, I think we sensed that we were dealing with a problem that was going to require more than just a let's-get-out-there-and-work-harder sort of response.'*

This is where strategic thinking starts – someone says 'Hold on a minute'. In other words, let's *not* just take action. Let's *not* just re-double our efforts or push the pressure down the ladder or tell our people to get out there and work harder. Let's *think* about this.

That seems to be Step Number 1. It is second nature, for most of us, when faced with a problem, to think automatically in terms of *doing* something about it. What should I *do* to solve this?

What we have to do, if we're going to think strategically, is shift the focus from action to understanding. Action will come later. What we're saying is that we'll focus, first, on *understanding*. Then, later, we'll turn our attention to action-taking.

Step 2 – stand back

But what do we think *about*? The secret, according to Jennifer Adair, is to discern the *patterns* in the problems coming to our attention.

*'If a single customer calls in with a specific complaint, then we've
got a one-off problem that we have to deal with. If three customers
call in with the same complaint, then we have a pattern. That's
when we have to start thinking strategically. There's something
going on here, and we have to figure out what it is. Our top reps
spot the patterns earlier – which is the key – and they can usually
figure them out more quickly.'*

In *every* problem-solving situation we have to get at the *real*
problem before we venture too far into the problem-solving cycle.
Unless we get down to the root causes, our efforts to remedy the
situation are quite likely to be misdirected and futile.

When it comes to discerning patterns, however, the notion of
unearthing the *root* problem doesn't quite fit. What's wrong is the
language. It suggests that we bombard the problem with our
what-where-when-who-why questions until we are able to ferret
out the underlying causes.

In truth, however, thinking strategically seems to require an
opposite sort of approach. What we need to do is stand *back* from
the problem and view it from a more *general* plane. The secret to
seeing a pattern is to move *back* and view the immediate problem
within its larger context.

If we do that we begin to see that the problem is part of a larger
pattern. This is what we mean by seeing the problem in its total
context. Our visit in Chapter 5 ended with the problem being
defined in the following manner:

> *Sales are down because our customers are changing their buying
> habits. Their decisions are being driven increasingly by economic
> factors, and the decision-making process itself has become
> increasingly centralised. Buying groups have entered into the mix
> in a fairly significant way. In those accounts where we have a Key
> Account Management strategy in place. Across the board,
> however, sales are down. We need to take a long, hard look at
> how the industry is changing and at the implications thereof for
> our own approach to doing business.*

The problem, then, is not just the fact that sales are down. That, as
it turns out, is just a symptom. The real issue has to do with some
rather fundamental questions of change and adaptation and
strategy.

Notice how our definition of the problem now extends well beyond our own organisation. It includes our customers, our competition, buying groups, legislative pressures, the industry as a whole. That's what happens when we *stand back* – and that is precisely the reason for doing it.

Step 3 – re-frame the problem

> When we re-frame the problem as a Do-It problem rather than a Fix-It problem we shift from thinking reactively to thinking proactively.

When we stand back, clearly, we simultaneously move our thinking from the specific to the general, from the pieces on the chess board to the *pattern* on the board.

Step 3 involves *staying* on that general plane – and thinking ahead to see how we can solve the problem.

Think ahead to see. The phrasing is curious. In effect, it means that we play out, in our mind's eye, a successful resolution of the problem. We imagine ourselves being where we want to be, with the problem solved. And then we find words to describe how it was all done.

> *Once we had defined the problem in those terms, it became clear that we had to re-think our whole approach to the market. It's something we had been doing anyway, but not in any systematic way. What we realised is that we had to tighten up, and speed up, the process. Otherwise, we would get left behind by what was happening out in the marketplace.*

Notice how the original problem – lagging sales – has been re-worked. The challenge, now, is to 're-think our whole approach to the market'. We have re-framed the problem as a Do-It problem rather than a Fix-It problem. We have shifted from thinking reactively to thinking proactively.

What emerged from the re-thinking was a whole new approach to the marketplace.

> *The message that we tried to put out was simple. Let's worry about developing a rock-solid relationship with our customer. Let's get to the point where we're helping them deal with the*

complexities and uncertainties that they are facing. If we can focus on delivering solutions that meet those needs then our sales will take care of themselves.

That meant not just a change in people's *thinking*, but some corresponding and supportive organisational changes as well. During the ensuing months we developed a new account planning process that got us building strategic partnerships with our major customers. At the same time, we re-organised our sales organisation so that each of our top ten accounts had an Account Executive acting as the principal contact. So now – rather than a major customer being called on by five different reps we have a single team going in there with a single strategic plan.

So – let's summarise.

- *Stop and think:* we resist the natural temptation to move into action. Instead, we *stop* and *think*.
- *Stand back:* rather than digging in to the problem, we *stand back* and look at it within its total context.
- *Re-frame:* we re-frame the *Fix-It* problem as a *Do-It* problem.

Everyday problems

What about those of us who are not operating at the director level? Do we still have to worry about thinking 'strategically'? After all, the problems that cross our desk from one day to the next are going to be comparatively straightforward:

- Barbara is going to be late for the meeting.
- The people in Marketing don't understand the memo that we sent around.
- Kevin's presentation to the people at GKN got, at best, a lukewarm response.
- The stamping machine on Line Three is down.

These are basically one-off problems. They call for remedial action or – perhaps in the case of Barbara being late – no action at all.

Or … could we be wrong about that? Is there more here than meets the eye?

Barbara may have a *habit* of being late or the misunderstood memo may signal a fundamental problem in communicating across departmental boundaries.

That's the first step in thinking strategically; we assume that things aren't quite as straightforward as they might look on the surface. Specifically, we assume that what we're seeing is part of a *pattern*.

Let's take the problem of the people in marketing not understanding the memo that we sent around.

If it turns out that we're not talking the same language because in marketing they're focused on things like brand awareness while over here we look at things like inventory then we have a pattern on our hands.

This is where we switch from thinking *Fix-It* to thinking *Do-It*. It happens almost automatically when we stand back and view a problem in its larger context. The need to deal reactively with the immediate problem gives way to an opportunity to tackle – proactively – a much larger, broader, and more significant issue.

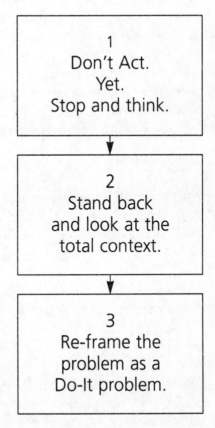

Fig. 26. Strategic thinking model.

The solution isn't to rush out and explain the memo to them. The bigger issue is that we have to break down the barriers that exist between departments within this company. When we're working on a key logistics issue why shouldn't someone from Marketing be seated at the table with us? When Marketing people are looking at pricing or planning a launch, why shouldn't they be getting input from someone in Logistics? Surely there are areas of overlap where the cross-fertilisation would produce a better result from a total *company* standpoint. We're thinking strategically.

Barriers to strategic thinking

In many cases, major corporations exercise strategy by default. IBM didn't consciously *choose* to remain *big* and almost fall by the wayside as smaller and more nimble competitors began to eat away at its core businesses. General Motors didn't consciously *choose* to stick with big cars with built-in style obsolescence while the Japanese and Germans opted for quality and timeless design and hit the Americans hard at both ends of the market.

No, they just kept on doing what they had always done, being the way they had always been. It's not a conscious strategic *choice*. It's a *lack* thereof.

Here are just a few of the reasons why it happens.

Success

Why change? We've always been successful doing things the way we do them. We've got a stranglehold on the marketplace. We spend more money on R&D than anyone else in the industry and we have four new products scheduled for launch this year. Why change?

Companies, of course, don't talk to themselves this way. No, the truth is that they don't talk to themselves at all. And that is precisely the problem. They operate on the basis of the above *assumptions*, which they leave unexamined and unchallenged. When the wake-up call finally arrives in the form of lagging sales and disappointed shareholders, the internal *causes* of the problem have generally reached an advanced state and major surgery may be the company's only remedial option.

Lack of success

> Who has time to sit back and think about strategy? We have to
> fight tooth and nail just to survive, going after whatever crumbs of
> business the big guys allow to slip off the table. All we can do is
> grab whatever business we can get.

Another common story, this time at the small, entrepreneurial
end of the marketplace. During their early start-up years, many
entrepreneurs make precisely the same mistake that IBM and
General Motors were guilty of. They operate blindly rather than
strategically. And, almost invariably, they suffer the same fate. By
the time the *Strategy Vacuum* problem shows itself in the form of
external symptoms, the internal organs are damaged almost
beyond repair.

Lack of time

> For individuals, as distinct from corporations, this is probably the
> Number One barrier. It would be *nice* to stand back and look at
> the Big Picture, but who the hell has time for it? In effect, that's
> what nine out of ten managers will tell you if you ask them
> why strategic thinking is being squeezed out of their busy
> schedules.

It raises the question, of course, as to why those other things are
more important than strategic thinking. Why it is *strategic
thinking* that is being squeezed out of the picture?

Crisis management

> It is difficult to address the strategic issues in a situation if we
> spend most of our day putting out fires and dealing with minor
> crises.

Tony Martindale again:

> *'I get twenty telephone calls a day, and heaven knows how many
> faxes. Every one of them is an urgent problem that I have to deal
> with. I've got trapped into this Fire-Fighting role to the point where
> that's how the customer sees me. I'm the guy that their store
> managers call when there's a problem. And you wonder why my
> boss rates me as not being very good at "addressing the strategic
> issues in this account".'*

The word *trapped* is a telling one – because that's what happens. Crisis management drowns out strategic thinking, and the absence of strategic thinking reinforces the need for more crisis management. And there are times when it seems that the only way to break out of this vicious cycle is to close the whole business down for a few days until we can get things *organised*! But the world won't allow us to do that. So we struggle on.

Concrete thinking

Some people have difficulty thinking in the abstract. They can recount, almost line for line and scene for scene, what happened in a movie they went to see on the weekend, but they have great difficulty summing the movie up in twenty-five words or less.

There seems to be a fairly tangible skill involved here. something which different people possess to varying degrees. People who *have* it are good at generalising, moving from the specific to the general and summarising.

People who *don't* have it tend to get bogged down in the details, tend to plod through things one step at a time.

A skillful chess player is able to see the chess board in a holistic fashion, to develop a keen *sense* for how the game is unfolding and what lies ahead. A gifted midfielder – David Beckham comes to mind – probably exercises much the same sort of skill. There's an uncanny sense of what is happening on the pitch, where the opportunities are ...

Unconscious assumptions

The nine-dot problem, which we examined earlier, is a good example of how an unconscious assumption takes the place of a strategy.

Volkswagen did a superb job, many years ago, of going against the unconscious assumption that an advertising campaign had to flaunt and trumpet a product's good points. Instead, in advertising the Beetle, Volkswagen poked fun at itself. Benson & Hedges did the same thing – and with equal success – when it launched the 100mm-length cigarette. The musical score associated with the Benson & Hedges ads, *The Disadvantages of You*, actually made it into the charts.

The unconscious assumption that ads have to be serious hinders strategic thinking by lulling us into thinking that we don't need to think strategically because there is only one strategy.

Remedy number 1: asking the right questions

One of the real secrets to thinking straight is simply to ask oneself the right questions. Here are some of the questions that we should routinely be asking ourselves.

What is going on here?

This is a good question to ask when we first look at a situation. Not *What do we do?* or even *What is wrong?* We may not have to 'do' anything. There may be nothing 'wrong'. Moving ahead on the basis of unconscious assumptions is deadly at *any* stage in the problem-solving process, and it is important that we avoid doing so right at the outset.

So we simply ask ourselves the most open-ended question that we can. *What is going on here?*

Is this part of a bigger problem?

Kevin's presentation to the people at GKN got, at best, a lukewarm response. That's a problem in itself, yes. And we have to deal with it. We'll have to sit down with Kevin to analyse where we missed the mark, and figure out what we can do to get the whole GKN proposal back on track.

But there's a bigger issue here. A 'pattern' issue. It has to do with Kevin's presentation skills. Doing presentations at the senior level is an absolutely vital part of Kevin's role, and it is something which he is not terribly good at. He doesn't *engage* people's thinking or bring his ideas to *life*.

Yes, we have to solve the immediate problem. But we also have to turn Kevin into a first-rate communicator who gets *through* to people.

Remedy number 2: getting away

Getting outside the work environment seems to help. This is

something we have talked about before – going to visit the pigeons and the squirrels.

Case study: Bryan Swindon

Bryan is one of Tony Martindale's bright young national account managers:

> *'When I was struggling to put together my annual plan for ASDA, Tony suggested that I take a couple of days and go off to Land's End or somewhere like that and really think about where I was going with the account and what I wanted to achieve. What he was saying, I think, was that I was thinking along lines that were too narrow, too detailed. I was having trouble standing back and looking at the bigger picture. And he was right. I didn't quite see how booking myself into a hotel at Land's End would solve the problem. In hindsight, however, it's one of the best things I've ever done. I ended up spending four days there.'*

Getting away from it all was part of the solution. But an equally important part had to do with what Bryan did while he was there.

> *'Tony talked to me about taking what he called a Back-from-the-Future approach. You think about where you'd like to be in, let's say, a year from now. You try to actually visualise how things are, or how they will be, as if you were actually there. And then you come back into the present and put together a plan that will take you from where you are now to where you were when you visited the future.'*

We'll come back to this point shortly. For now, however, let's let Bryan elaborate:

> *'In my case, it meant creating an image in my mind of the way I would be operating with ASDA a year from now – the sort of role I would be playing, the way I would be perceived, who I would be spending time with, the role that Tony and Michelle and the other people on the account team would be playing, the new products we'd be bringing out, the growth in ASDA's business ... everything.'*

Remedy number 3: thinking backwards

We've just seen this – in Bryan's deliberations down at Land's End. He called it a 'Back-from-the-Future' approach.

It is an especially useful tool when the solution to our problem involves someone other than ourselves. The problem might be to convince the executive committee to release funds for a project or encourage the people on our team to think more creatively about things. In these cases, the solution has to do with a reaction or behaviour that has to occur in *someone else*.

So we think backwards.

> *'Okay, I'm the hospital. I've decided to buy not just more sutures and drapes but a whole package of products cemented into a two-year contract. Now ... I did that because it lowered my costs. It reduced the number of orders that had to be processed and the number of decisions that had to be made. It saves money by allowing me to run things more efficiently at my end. And that's my Number One strategic objective. To stay in business. To get our costs down and avoid being a victim in the next round of closures.'*

Now, as the vendor, *selling* these products into the hospital, what does this tell me about my strategy?

> *'We got their business because we positioned ourselves as a means of cutting their administrative costs. We held out the promise of helping them achieve their Number One strategic objective.'*

We got their business because we positioned ourselves as – is a very, very important half-sentence. It's the first half of a *strategic* statement. If you complete it you are making a statement of strategy. It can't be helped. Here are some other examples of strategic half-statements:

- We got their approval because we demonstrated that ...
- I passed the test because I was able to ...
- We convinced them by presenting our idea as ...
- I got them on-side by showing them that ...
- I sold them the concept by packaging it as ...
- They brought the programme because they saw it as ...
- We won the contract because we showed them that ...
- We sold the deal by positioning it as a solution to ...

Complete any of these statements and what you end up with is a general approach. A way of *presenting* something that produced a favourable reaction from the other party. And that is precisely what we mean by the word 'strategy'. *We got their business because we positioned ourselves as …*

Remedy number 4: thinking pictorially

We talked about this under the heading of creativity. And our returning to it under this new heading reinforces the close tie between creative and strategic thinking.

There's an example of pictorial thinking in Figure 27. It's the same schematic we introduced near the outset of this book. Problem-solving, it says, can be thought of as a process comprised of six fundamental steps.

There are some really neat things about this diagram. It doesn't take up a lot of space. Indeed, it sums up in a few square inches what might take a whole *chapter* of text to properly describe. The diagram captures the *dynamic* of problem-solving … the process, the movement. It does a better job than mere words would do because diagrams are fundamentally non-linear media whereas text is a distinctly *linear* medium. The diagram is easy to remember – much easier than pages and pages of text. If we were conducting a training workshop on problem-solving then this diagram would serve our purpose much more effectively than anything we could find in textual form.

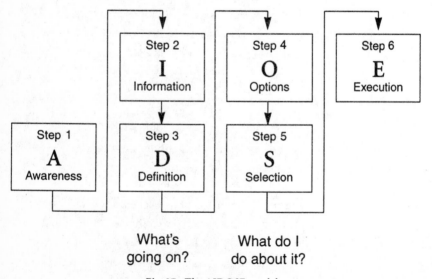

Fig. 27. The AIDOSE model.

Remedy number 5: talking to someone

It helps to talk. You might recall the case of Susan, charged with
the task of putting together a resource library for her company's
sales and marketing division:

> *'Talking it through with Tony was a critical turning point. Rather
> than being in the library – up to my ears with it, in fact – talking
> with Tony allowed me to see it as an outsider would see it. To get
> a sense of perspective about the whole thing. To look at it from
> the standpoint of other people – not just Tony, but the people in
> the various departments under Tony.'*

Remedy number 6: explaining it to the bank manager

As a last resort, take two simple steps.

- Imagine that you own the company.
- Imagine that you have to explain what you are doing to your
  bank manager.

This is the problem I am wrestling with, this is why I think
it's important, this is the strategy I've been using to tackle it,
these are the options I've looked at, and this is where I am right
now.

Summary

In this chapter as before we have looked at the importance of strategic
thinking in the problem-solving process.

- The concept of *strategic thinking* gets to the heart of what
  effective problem-solving is all about.
- A strategy isn't a goal or an action plan. It's a *way* of tackling a
  problem or working toward an objective.
- If we're going to think strategically we shift the focus from
  action to understanding. We have to resist the urge to *do*
  something.
- The first step is to assume that things aren't quite as straightforward as they look – that the problem we're seeing is part of
  a larger *pattern*.
- We need to stand *back* from the problem – rise *above* it, view it
  from a more *general* plane.

- Then we re-frame the problem as a Do-It problem rather than a Fix-It problem. We shift from thinking reactively to thinking proactively.
- The need to deal reactively with the immediate problem gives way to an opportunity to tackle – proactively – a larger and more significant issue.

CHAPTER 12

Selling the Solution

R arely can a solution be implemented – and the problem solved – without our having to get the buy-in and co-operation of other people.

For some people, the notion of having to 'sell' their ideas sounds vaguely disreputable – the sort of thing one shouldn't have to do if the ideas are sound and their audience is intelligent and willing to look at things in a logical and objective manner.

Case study: Graeme Weir _____

Graeme Weir, one of our *Famous Five*, had this to say:

> '*I remember taking one of my people aside after he had done a presentation to the directors, trying to convince us of the merits of investing in a new control system for the warehouse. He had probably spent a good three or four days putting together a written proposal which he had circulated to the directors prior to the meeting. The proposal was superb. It covered everything the directors needed to know and it answered all the questions. It laid all the data out in a very compelling manner. But his verbal presentation was rather flat. He kept referring to arguments and data that were contained in the proposal, and he seemed to lose the audience early on. He never did quite grab their interest.*'

The problem?

> '*No one had read the proposal. I did – but I'm an engineer, and I do that sort of thing. Besides, this was one of my people. But no one else had read it. That's not how they make decisions. They want someone to get up and talk to them, and sell them the idea – not bore them with technical detail or insist that they find time to read through a rather detailed proposal when they have a zillion other things to do. They're willing to buy ... but they want to be sold.*' _____

The lesson is this. If we're going to get a solution implemented, and if it needs the wholehearted co-operation from some of the people around us, then it has to be sound. It has to make sense.

But it also has to be sold.

In this chapter, we're going to take a close-up look at five different aspects of selling our solution:

- Being proactive.
- Mapping the decision.
- Going in well-prepared.
- Convincing people on the fly.
- Overcoming resistance to change.

Being proactive: you have to make it happen

Case study: Jennifer Adair _____

Jennifer was talking recently about the training and development needs of her company's up-and-coming middle managers.

> 'The single biggest stumbling block is the inability to sell internally. If you have an idea, or you need to get something approved, you have to know how decisions are made and who is involved. And you have to manage the whole process. You have to make it happen. If you just plop the idea on someone's desk and then stand back and wait for something to happen, it's not going to. You have to be proactive.'

Proactive. It's a crucial word. Managing the process. Not taking things for granted.

There are also some very important interpersonal *skills* involved here. Back to Jennifer.

> 'You have to know how to approach people. They have their own schedules and their own priorities – to the point where you sometimes wonder whether we're all working for the same company. But that's reality, and you have to work with it. You have to win people over. You have to show them the pay-off for helping out. You have to sell them on the idea of their getting involved in your project or team.' _____

We'll be talking about some of the skills later. For now, however, let's underscore the importance of having the right attitude. As Jennifer says, you *have to be proactive.*

That means a number of things. It means recognising that no one cares as much about your proposed solution as you do. It means recognising that, when push comes to shove and a little nudge is what's needed to get a solution back on track, that nudge will have to come from you.

> You have to be proactive. You have to champion the solution and make it happen.

No one cares as much about your proposed solution as you do. That's another one of those *mantras* that we should repeat to ourselves until we get sick of hearing it. You have to champion the solution and make it happen.

Mapping the decision

If the implementation of your solution needs to be approved by others – if a *decision* is needed, in other words – then you have to take responsibility for managing the decision-making process. And the most important step of all is simply to *understand* the decision-making process.

- Who exactly will be involved in the making of the decision, and at what specific stage?
- What specific role will each person play in the decision-making process?
- What will each person be looking for? What criteria will they apply to the decision?
- How do they perceive and feel about your proposed solution right now?

Decisions are rarely made by a single person, operating in total isolation. Judy might be *making* the decision, but she will no doubt want to consult with John and Karen before making a final commitment. She might even have to have a chat with Mary Ward if the cost of the proposal is going to go much beyond the £5,000 mark.

These are the people, and the process, that you have to influence in order to ensure that your proposed solution gets the commitment you are looking for.

What criteria will determine whether their bottom-line is a thumbs-up or a thumbs-down? In the case of Mary Ward, it might be a fairly straightforward matter of costs and payback. But how about the others? What exactly will persuade them that the solution is worth going ahead with?

And – how do they see your proposal right *now*? At each point in the decision-making process, each of the key players will have a certain perception of your proposed solution and a certain reaction to it, and it would be ideal if we (1) knew what that perception and reaction was and (2) had a plan for moving it towards the enthusiastic end of the continuum.

These are tough questions, and tough challenges. You might have to talk directly to John or Karen or Sabrina on a one-to-one basis. At the very least, there are clearly some things here that you will have to think about.

- ◆ If a brief chat with Judy reveals that she hasn't even thought about the decision yet, what is the best way to make it happen?
- ◆ Mary Ward is the one who has to actually sign the cheque. If she is sceptical, or disinterested, that is something you need to know about.
- ◆ John will probably try to shoot your proposal down because that's just the way he is. How will you deal with that?
- ◆ Sabrina is an unknown. She's new but she is well-regarded by the research group in Texas. We'll need to find out more about her and the role she plays.

That's the kind of proactive thinking and planning we have to be doing in order to manage the decision-making process as best we can.

Going in well-prepared

In many situations, the selling of a solution takes place in the form of a formal or semi-formal presentation. However it is done, the key thing is that you have time to fine-tune your arguments and develop a convincing presentation.

Preparation is the key. It is largely a matter of covering the right questions, and then doing the homework needed to answer those questions in as comprehensive a fashion as possible.

Let's go through some of those questions now.

What is needed?

People in the audience have to be aware of the need before we can sell them a solution to it. If people are unclear about what the issue is, then they will not be in a position to recognise and 'buy' the rationale behind your solution. Never assume that people understand. Spell it out.

What has been tried before?

If we are proposing a solution that has been tackled before, we need to go in with a thorough understanding of what has been done in the past. There is nothing more damaging than to have someone say –

> 'Didn't we try something like that last April? It seems to me that there was a programme over in Jack's area ...'

– and to have to admit that we're not aware of that incident. Jack's dismal failure will damage our own proposal unless we can demonstrate exactly how and why our solution is better.

What are the other options?

We have to let people know that we have considered other options. They will know that there are various solutions we could have come up with. We have to let them know that we have looked at the options very carefully, and settled on one that will best capitalise on the opportunity.

What are others doing?

People will want to know how our competitors are handling this problem. How is it that the Wilson people, whose products aren't as *good* as ours, have managed to avoid being hit by the problem? Baxter struggled with this issue for a whole year; what did *they* end up doing?

You have to have answers for these questions, because they will be on people's minds. Executives pay a lot of attention to their competitors and what successful companies in other industries are doing. They don't like reinventing the wheel or playing catch-up.

If someone else has found a solution to the problem let's find out what they did and then do it better.

How would we proceed?

Assuming we adopt the solution, how exactly would we proceed? Who would be involved? How would the project be managed? How much would it cost? When, exactly, would you recommend that we get started?

At some point, if we have done a good job of selling the proposed solution, people are going to want answers to these questions. They will come later in the discussion rather than sooner, and you have to have the answers available. We can't afford to fumble the ball at this stage, and we don't want to have to improvise and end up committing ourselves to a plan of action that comes back to haunt us later.

Getting people involved

There are times when the key to getting your solution implemented can be the impromptu meeting in the hallway – getting Jim to take a look at a proposal before you send it upstairs, getting June to let you borrow two of her people, convincing Charles that his presence at the Tuesday meeting is vital.

These people all have their own busy schedules and their own priorities and, just like you, they have to keep the boss happy. The priorities of someone in Accounting are never going to overlap with yours and there is no point in beating people over the head with the old adage that we all have to do is what's good for the customer.

No, the idea of their involvement is something that has to be *sold*. Here's how we can do it.

Build a network

It helps to be well-liked. It is always easier – when you need something done – to have developed a network of people around the company whose time and attention you can call upon when you need it. People who will take time out from their busy schedules to lend a hand simply because they like you, and want to help you succeed, and think you're a good person, and appreciate the fact that you would do the same for them and have in *fact* done so in the past.

How do you earn that type of reputation? Most often, it comes down to the small things:

- Greet people with a cheery 'Good morning'.
- Don't hide in your office during the lunch hour.
- Join your colleagues at the pub on Friday afternoon.
- Stop and get Jennifer a 'Get Well' card.
- Congratulate Arthur on his appointment.
- Express enthusiasm for Gloria's proposal.
- See if Jack needs any help with his project.

Acknowledge their priorities

> *'I know you've got a busy afternoon ahead of you, Frank, but I wonder if I can just get a couple of pieces of information from you.'*

That's a good way of letting Frank know that *we* know he has lots of other things to do. It's not just a matter of common courtesy. It's also a good example of the old selling strategy – taking the customer's most likely objection, voicing it before he or she has a chance to do so, and then sweeping it off the table.

Look and sound like a winner

People like to be associated with a winner. If you've managed to chalk up a series of successes, then you will undoubtedly find that people are becoming more and more willing to give you the time and attention you need from them. You don't need to twist their arms the way you used to.

If you sound like a non-winner, on the other hand – if there's an apologetic tone to your voice – then you're going to have to twist their arms if you hope to get them involved. They certainly aren't going to come along willingly.

Be explicit about what you want – and why

> *'What I need, Gord, is some marketing input. We need someone on the team who can relate what we're trying to do here to what's*

been done in the US – and I figure you're the ideal person to bring that kind of perspective to the table.'

And that, Gord, is why I need you on the team. Spell it out. And do it in a positive way that pinpoints the specific value that Gord's presence will add to the team.

Spell out the benefits

There has to be *something* in the way of a benefit or a payoff. Think carefully about this beforehand. Put yourself in the other person's shoes. Think it through from his or her vantage point. *What's in it for me?*

> *'This might be a good chance for you to see, Judy, how all this data you generate is being used at the sharp end of the business.*
> *It'll be good exposure for you, Jack. Howard and Maureen are both going to be there, and they'll be paying particular attention to this issue.'*

Resistance to change

Let's spend a bit of time talking about resistance to change. There are times when the solution we have proposed is going to affect a large number of people. And that is when we encounter a widespread resistance to anything that is different to the way things have been done for the last twenty years.

It doesn't happen as much as it used to. And that's simply because there aren't too many people which have not been hit by *some* sort of fairly radical change during the past decade or so.

So people have become more accustomed to change but that doesn't mean that they are *embracing* it. It's more a matter of resignation than a sign that people are throwing themselves wholeheartedly into an effort to make such changes successful.

Let's examine, briefly, some of the myths that surround this whole issue of resistance to change.

People don't like new technology

That's nonsense, of course. The people who resist the introduction of new technology are the same ones who buy the latest electronic and hi-fi equipment at Currys or Dixons. So long as we're talking about video machines that let you record your favourite soap at the press of a button then the average person doesn't seem to have any real problem with new technology or the introduction of change.

A good idea will sell itself

Perhaps a good idea should sell itself. But it doesn't.

There are lots of good ideas around. In magazines, on the internet, in books, on audio tapes. But none of these make much of a dent in our thinking or the way we do things. It is only when a specific idea can be related to a specific need that we really pay attention to an idea.

And that's not something that can happen passively. It's the *selling* of the idea that penetrates the barrier of disinterest.

There is, indeed, an irony here. There are times when a *poorer* idea is more apt to be adopted than a *better* idea because more work has been put into packaging and selling it. As a result it's *talked* about rather than left gathering dust on the shelf. People *think* about it. And it ends up, perhaps with a few modifications, being accepted. The superior idea, having been presented passively in the form of a proposal or report, sits untouched.

People read things we give them to read

'I don't know why they're having trouble understanding the change to the security codes; that was explained in the outline we sent around.'

People don't read outlines or manuals that we send around. Anything longer than a few lines is unlikely to be read by more than two or three people out of twenty. The average person, let's not forget, has only a handful of books in their house and is more likely to leaf through a single tabloid every day than pick up the *Financial Times*. Most people aren't readers by nature.

So we can never assume that something has been read, or understood, just because it has been 'sent around'.

Resistance has to be 'overcome'

The very word 'resistance' has an adversarial colouring to it. It clearly implies that *we* – the progressive thinkers – are trying to move ahead and *they* – the ones who are afraid of change – are an obstacle standing in our way. So part of our planning has to be a strategy for *overcoming* that resistance.

And that, of course, is almost *asking* for trouble. With such an adversarial outlook in our minds we leave the other side out of the early discussions. We don't consult them or work with them.

If there *is* resistance to change, then it is important that we look upon it in a fundamentally *positive* manner – as a useful red flag, as a signal that something needs a bit more care and attention.

Right from the start

There's no point in spending hours analysing a problem and developing a solution if your superiors have already decided upon another way of dealing with the situation.

Nor, indeed, do you want to propose a solution that has no chance of gaining the support of certain key directors because they rejected a similar proposal last autumn.

The point is this. We shouldn't look at 'selling the solution' at the tail-end of the problem-solving process. It is something you should be thinking about right from the start.

Summary

In this chapter we looked at the process of selling the solution to those who matter.

- ◆ Good ideas don't sell themselves. They have to be good. They have to make sense.
- ◆ No one cares as much about your proposed solution as you do.
- ◆ You have to be proactive. You have to champion the solution and make it happen.
- ◆ You need a clear understanding of the total decision-making process that will decide whether your solution is accepted or rejected.
- ◆ Who is involved? How do they perceive and feel about our proposal?

- A single presentation can make or break our case. The key here is *preparation* – knowing what questions count, and having answers for them.
- We also have to know how to get individual people involved. It helps, for one thing, to have a 'network' in place.
- Recognise that people have their own concerns and their own busy schedules – and let them *know* that you recognise it.
- Look and sound like a winner. Don't sound apologetic or diffident when you ask for people's involvement.
- Be explicit about what you want – and why. Tell each person in a positive way what specific value he or she will add to the total effort.
- Spell out the benefits. *What's in it for them?* What exactly do they have to gain by getting involved?
- Don't leave it too late. Get out there and start selling.

Managerial Problem-Solving

*The whole thrust of
our job is to
impact on the way
things are done by
those around us.*

M anagers, as problem-solvers, have to walk a very fine line. And leverage – understanding it, finding it, creating it – is the name of the game.

By and large, this book is about *you* as a problem-solver. Our aim has been to maximise the results which you get when you tackle problems.

You as a manager

We also have to look, of course, at you as a *manager*. And we're going to define the word 'manager' fairly broadly here. If you have people reporting to you then you are, by definition, a manager. That's the conventional definition. These days, however, a lot of us are being paid to provide leadership without having formal 'authority' and without having people 'report' to us. The whole thrust of our job is to impact on the way things are done by those around us.

So if you don't have staff reporting to you and if you don't have the word 'manager' in your title, but if you're being paid to exercise the sort of influence just alluded to, then consider yourself a *manager*. This chapter is for you.

We're still dealing with *you* as a problem-solver. But, we need to look at problem solving from a *managerial* point of view, and that is what we are going to do in this chapter.

The concept of leverage

Leverage is what defines a managerial role as 'managerial'.

The first thing we have to do is understand the concept of

leverage. Leverage – not the number of people reporting into you – is what defines a managerial role as 'managerial'.

Or at least *potential* leverage, because not all managers exercise the leverage inherent in their roles. The successful ones do and that is what defines their success as managers.

Leverage is what you get when you use a pulley system to control the boom on a sailboat rather than a single rope. It multiplies the amount of *power* you can generate.

Leverage is what managers use to produce results which go far beyond anything we could produce acting on our own. By training someone, by influencing people's attitudes, by developing tools which other people can use, we are exercising leverage. We are wielding an influence that extends farther and deeper than anything we could produce if we were acting solely on our own.

If, on the other hand, we say 'Move over, Jim, let me see if I can figure it out', then we're *not* exercising leverage. We're just operating as a single employee solving a single problem. We're standing in for Jim.

That might be valuable. We may solve an important problem. It may allow things to move ahead. But it's not leverage.

As managers, leverage is what we have to aim for. Given the scarcity of time at our disposal, given the rate at which things evolve and priorities change and problems emerge, we can't afford to do anything less than exercise leverage.

> As managers, leverage is what we have to aim for. In everything we do.

Directing – the natural impulse

Let's take some typical problems that might come to our attention as managers:

- One of your people has a crucial meeting tomorrow with a major supplier. You've asked them to come in and talk things over.
- One of your people has called *you* and asked for some time. They are wrestling with a problem and would like some input.
- A customer is furious, and is threatening to cancel an important programme. You're still not quite sure what's happened.

♦ Judy is giving a major presentation to the Executive Committee in a couple of days. There's a whole year's worth of planning at stake.

These are all important situations in that something has to be discussed and decided. And, in most cases, time is of the essence.

The *old* way of managing is to step in and do people's thinking for them.

♦ Just get whatever you have out on the truck, Mark. There's no point in having it go out half-empty. The rest of the packing can wait.

♦ Leave the ad work for now, Judy. They'll survive without you. Call Hendricks and set something up for tomorrow. Tell him that you've got some new data that …

♦ I think what we need to do, Jill, is take a more aggressive approach. Let's let them know that we're sure of our ground and have no intention of backing off.

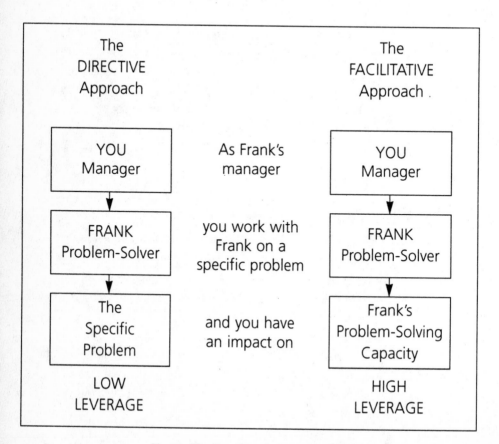

Fig. 28. The directive v facilitative model.

Let's acknowledge something very important – these ways of reacting are very *natural*. We solve the problem for them.

We'll call this the *directive* approach to managing. That doesn't mean authoritarian. It simply means that we are, with the very best of intentions, trying to be helpful by offering a solution to the problem.

There are, however, some pitfalls when we do this.

- *You have to be there.* If you're tied up in a meeting, or at home in bed with the flu, then the problem isn't going to get solved in the way you would like.
- *No learning occurs.* They may learn a bit, by simply seeing what specific solution you came up with – but they don't learn much about the actual problem-solving *process*.
- *You may be wrong.* Or, more likely, it may be less than optimal. What looks right from your managerial perch may, when seen from ground level, not be the best solution at all.

The big problem is the fact that the person doesn't learn anything. In other words, there's no *leverage*. You haven't left the other person better equipped to solve the *next* problem. And that is a brand of management that you can't afford to be practising. Not these days.

Facilitating – the better way

Let's compare the *directive* way of managing to a better way. The *facilitative* way.

The situation is this – Frank comes to us with a decision he has to make. We want to make sure that he's going to handle it in an optimal fashion.

We start off with an important assumption. *Frank is capable of solving this problem. I don't have to solve it for him. I just have to give him a little help.*

Given a chance to sit down and talk about it most people are quite capable of solving their own problems. Unless we're prepared to make that assumption, we lock ourselves into a directive mode of managing which ultimately dooms us to failure as managers.

But Frank does need help. Otherwise, he would have come up with a workable and realistic solution when you said, 'Frank, we've got a problem here; what are we going to do about it?' He needs some help.

Still – the fact remains. For the problem to be solved effectively Frank has to come up with the solution himself. People learn best when they arrive at the solution themselves. Our job, as managers, is to help them do that.

Our value-added contribution

Let's be quite precise about what we can do to facilitate. We want to enhance Frank's solution of the problem or the decision he makes. What is it, precisely, that we as managers bring to the process?

The wisdom of experience

We probably have more years under our belt. We know the system better. We've had more dealings with the people at corporate office. We've seen more and done more and heard more.

- So we've seen what works and what doesn't. We might just save Frank some time and energy.
- We can add the pragmatism that comes with experience, a feel for what's possible and what's not.
- We probably have a better sense of perspective and proportion – we're less apt to get flustered by a problem.

A sounding board

We bring a sounding board to bear on the process of problem-solving. Frank will be able to talk things through rather than think things through – and that's a lot more effective.

- Having to put his thoughts in words forces him to be logical and coherent. Ideas that he might have thought were clear will really become clear once he has put them into words.
- Hearing them spoken aloud will give him a sense of objectivity. Nothing helps a person think things through clearly more than the need to puts one's thoughts into words.

Ideas and suggestions

Two heads are better than one. We may have something specific to add to the problem-solving process – an idea, some insight into one of the key players. And we are uniquely positioned to add background information, inside information, the sort of stuff that comes with our greater experience and knowledge of the 'system'.

Someone to argue with

Even if all we do is argue with Frank, at least we'll be forcing him to marshal his facts, find ways to rebut or refute our arguments, and so on. If there is any looseness in his thinking, he will be forced to tighten it up. He'll come away better prepared for any adversarial encounters that might be awaiting him as he moves forward with his plan for solving the problem.

The magic of asking questions

Let's talk now about *how* we add value.

As a means of *shaping* the way people think and directing their thinking along lines that we *know* will be productive ... nothing is as powerful as the simple expedient of asking a question.

> A good question not only *activates* the person's thinking but actually *directs* it along lines which we suspect will be productive.

A question – *What exactly are we trying to achieve here?* – is basically an invitation for the other person to *think*. But, used skilfully, it can do more than that. It not only *activates* the person's thinking but actually *directs* it along lines which we suspect will be productive. To be precise, the adroit use of questions can help us – as Frank's manager – to help *Frank* think:

- Logically
- Broadly
- Incisively
- Resourcefully
- Creatively
- Boldly
- Realistically
- Empathically
- Proactively
- Decisively

Let's look at how it's done.

1. *Logically*

This is one of two fundamental dimensions that we have to be concerned about:

- *Thinking horizontally.* Thinking logically about the outcomes of an action. In effect, thinking horizontally across the time plane.
- *Thinking vertically.* Moving from the specific level to the general. Thinking in systems terms. Thinking about the other people or components or forces involved.

First, the *horizontal.* We want Frank to *think* about cause-and-effect. What leads to what? We want him to think *logically.*

> 'Okay, Frank, but let's think about that a bit. You do this or that. What's going to happen then?'

In effect, we want him to *project* his thinking into the future. We want him to see, in his mind's eye, the chain of causes and effects that is likely to unfold if he takes a specific action.

You may have to play a more directive role, bringing in *your* experience and insights, if he thinks through cause-effect relationships and doesn't see an outcome that you know is there.

First, though, try to get *him* to see it.

> 'Okay, Frank, that's his reaction on day 1. Think for a minute about day 2. He's back in his office, and he's got his pocket calculator out and he's adding up the figures ...'

You're asking him to think along certain channels without telling him what he's going to find when he does. Your helpfulness, your value added, stems from the simple fact of *directing* his thinking.

2. *Broadly*

Vertically now. Here, our aim is to *elevate* his thinking to a higher plane – to help him stand back and take a more encompassing view of the situation.

We want him to see how things interconnect, how a change in one part of the overall system will have an impact on other parts of the system.

'Okay, Frank, but let's look at the other players involved. What's their stake in all this, and how are they likely to react?'

Or, *'That might solve our problem, Frank, but let's look at it from the retailer's standpoint. What are the other priorities he has on his mind?'*

One of the most difficult things for a subordinate to do is to look at all sides of a problem with objectivity. The closer we are to a situation, the less likely we are to see all sides of it. We may make a decision that seems quite logical and realistic as we see it but may be less than optimal, even *wrong*, when looked at from a broader perspective.

As managers, we can bring a sense of perspective to bear. To do so, however, we have to remain in our managerial role. If we look at it too much from the *subordinate's* point of view then the advantages of our broader perspective can easily be dissipated.

3. Incisively

One of the most useful things we can do is help people boil things down to the essentials.. By asking a question:

- *Okay, Bill, what's the most important single thing we have to achieve in this situation?*
- *Jack, you've given me three pages with lots and lots of words. What we need is a one-page list of numbers that shows how we're adding value to the customer's bottom line.*
- *Judy, these are all great ideas ... but what is it precisely that you want Bob to commit to?*

There's always a danger of failing to define the problem properly before trying to decide what to do about it. There's a real danger of jumping to conclusions and we end up treating the symptoms only and not coming to grips with the real and more basic problem.

'Okay, Frank. Let's take a deep breath and ask ourselves – what's the real issue here?'

Let's take a deep breath. This suggests taking a break, looking at things holistically. Because that's what Frank has to do. And once he's done that he has to answer a specific question. What's the real issue here?

4. Resourcefully

Who *else* should be involved? What does Frank need to learn from other people? Whose help will he need? Whose support?

Our aim here – and again, we achieve it primarily through asking questions – is to encourage Frank to make full and optimal use of the resources which we, as a company, can offer. That's what being *resourceful* means. Making do with what you've got.

> 'Let me raise a question, Frank. Are you the person who should be dealing with this problem? And, if you are, are there other people you need to get involved?'

5. Creatively

Are there any other approaches we might want to consider? That's the issue we have to raise here.

Okay, can you think of any other way we could play this?

Here, we're trying to channel Frank's thinking process along innovative lines. We're inviting him to think of something new and different.

- How about ...?
- What about ...?
- Have you thought about ...?
- What would happen if ...?

We're putting specific action options out on the table – but gently, in question form. We're trying to get Frank to fit it into his own scheme of thinking.

> 'What would happen if we simply did nothing? Is that an alternative we should consider?'

Try this on (Action) and see where it leads you (Outcomes). Look at the outcomes that this action would produce. We're phrasing it as a question. We're asking him to *think*.

Notice that we don't just say *I think you should* do this or that.

Why not? For one thing, there may be a practical flaw in the idea that we are not aware of but that he will see from his ground-level perspective. He, after all, is the one who actually has to execute.

Secondly, and more importantly, he has to make it his own idea in order for it to work. It has to be his – because it will invariably have to be tailored to suit the unfolding situation. It will have to be done at the propitious time and in a propitious manner and it has to sound like him.

6. *Boldly*

If we sense he's shying away from something, we say,

> '*Hold on, Frank ... What's the worst thing that could happen? What's the down side? What's the up side? Let's weigh the two ...*'

Our focus here is on helping Frank weigh the dangers and payoffs. If we sense he's confining his thinking to low-risk options, we might encourage him to examine bolder strategies. Or, if he is thinking along risk-laden lines, we'll want to make sure that he has made a realistic effort to weigh the pros and cons.

> '*I wonder if that's as risky as it sounds, Frank. Let's think it through ...*'

In effect, we're tailoring our contribution to what we hear Frank saying – and to what we know about his inclination or disinclination to take risks.

7. *Realistically*

We want Frank to think realistically about what's possible and what's not. We want him to assume that, as a rule, things take a lot longer than one might reasonably expect.

So we issue a warning. In the form, again, of a question.

> '*You're assuming that these guys are going to go along with you, but I wonder ... Will they? What have we seen in the past?*'

8. Empathically

We want Frank to put himself in the customer's shoes. And this applies both to a customer who buys our products or services or an *internal* customer – someone down the hall.

> 'Frank. If you're the customer … What's important to you? What do you need to see and hear? Do it consciously, Frank … pretend you're the customer.'

9. Proactively

What can we do to influence things? Where's our *leverage*? Far too often, people do all the right things to campaign for the result they want – and then stop. We don't want Frank to stop. We want him to be always looking for ways to make things happen.

- What can we do …?
- Where's our leverage …?
- How can we keep the ball rolling …?
- How can we make it happen …?
- How can we steer the course of events …?
- How can we influence what he thinks or does …?
- How can we prevent that from happening …?

Again, the trick for you as a manager is to ask questions. The answers aren't terribly difficult to find …

10. Decisively

We want Frank to be action-driven. Even though he's defining the problem first and then exploring alternate solutions, we want there to be a little voice in the back of his mind always asking *What are you going to do and when are you going to do it?*

Those are challenging questions. Asking them is one of the most useful things we can do as managers.

Looking for leverage

Our biggest challenge as managers is to exercise every ounce of *leverage* that we can. The more leverage we exercise, the more *effective* we are as managers, and the more value we add to the organisation that is paying our wages.

Being aware of time

Time – or, more to the point, a *lack* of time – is the enemy. We would do well to keep *reminding* ourselves of that fact again and again as we work through the average week. We have to keep reminding ourselves – I have to make conscious and intelligent decisions about what to do with the limited amount of time that I have at my disposal.

Thinking 'investment'

As managers we have to look for *leverage*. We have to involve ourselves in those problems and issues where our specific skills and insight will make a difference.

Case study: Susan McTaggart ───────────────────────

Susan McTaggart, one of our *Famous Five*, had this to say:

> *'I think of my time as being "invested" in things. So I'm always asking myself – Is this a good investment? Is there a significant benefit to be gained here? How large is the payoff compared to what it would be if I did this ... or this ... or this? I don't spend a lot of time exploring these issues; it's more like a quick computation that I do in my head, automatically, every time I have to choose what to do next.'*

The problem that a lot of us have, of course, is that we aren't actively *choosing* what to do next. Too often, we're reacting to events as they unfold. We're being *reactive* rather than *proactive* in terms of how we allocate our time. We're not making conscious *decisions*. ──────────────────

The challenge is to bring our *usage* of time under our direct and conscious control. By making conscious, intelligent decisions. By investing our time wisely.

Keeping informed

Time and time again, observers have found that successful executives keep themselves well informed about what is going on around them.

Getting *good* information is always a challenge. There are going to be some people whose opinions you can count on. For the most part, however, it's best to assume that people are going to be somewhat self-serving in how they convey information and opinion to you.

We need to recognise the importance of being in touch with what is happening, cultivate our sources, and take a discerning approach to assessing what we hear through those sources.

Case study: Tony Martindale _____

'I always know that with Andrea (Tony's Human Resources director), I'll always get an honest – sometimes brutally honest – appraisal of things. And that's something I appreciate. If I need to bounce an idea around, or discuss something off the record, or think out loud about a very difficult decision involving someone on staff, I always know I can do it with Andrea. She's a great sounding board, and she's not afraid to pull me up if I'm waffling or not making any sense.' _____

Reserving time for 'walking around'

Don't allow all of your time to get tied up with meetings, appointments, presentations or luncheons. You should reserve a significant chunk of time every day for 'managing by walking around'.

It's your only opportunity to get a *feel* for what is happening, to sense the *mood* of the team, and – importantly – to give people a chance to bring information or problems to your attention.

Moving in and out of situations

As we're 'managing by walking around', we are invariably going to come across some problems. Some of them will be juicy, here-and-now problems that invite us to roll our sleeves up and feel useful. And it is difficult at times to know whether to plunge in with both feet, studiously avoid getting involved, or seek out some sort of middle ground.

Getting the balance right is tricky. If you have ever watched a good primary school teacher in action – one teacher against a class of thirty or so high-energy toddlers – you will have seen how it ought to be done. No, you don't plunge in with both feet. You stop at this table just long enough to lavish praise then you go on to the next table to stop an argument and then you see if there are any other crises that demand immediate attention before visiting the table where Jeremy and Paul have just spilt a can of paste over Lucy's uniform …

This is multi-tasking at its most demanding. It represents a pattern of managerial behaviour which most of us should be striving to emulate. A work of advice. A quick question. A pat on the back. A two-minute consultation. Good managers linger just long enough to make a difference. And then they keep moving.

Linking the specific to the general

When senior managers talk about problems, they often shift back and forth between the specific and the general.

> *Jim is after me to set up a committee to look at whether we belong in the home care market. That's the kind of decision we don't seem to make very well around here. We're superb on the operational stuff; but when it comes to the directional issues, the wheels seem to spin forever unless I step in.*

There's a specific issue that has to be resolved, having to do with the home care market. And it looks as if our unnamed executive will be involved, albeit grudgingly, in making that decision. Of equal interest, though, is the telling comment – *That's the kind of decision we don't seem to make very well around here.* That observation has to do with *process.* It has to do with a general tendency of which the home care decision is but a single manifestation.

> That's the sort of thinking that a high-leverage manager has to be doing all the time. Looking for the patterns, refusing to deal with problems in isolation, reserving his or her attention for those higher-level issues which cut across divisions and departments and functions.

This is a sophisticated form of leverage which we find in experienced senior managers. They think about problems on two different levels, and they will be willing to spend time on a specific problem precisely because it lends itself to that sort of dual-layered approach. A problem involving product quality, for example, becomes interesting because it is tied to a larger concern about the efficacy of production control systems.

A high-leverage manager is always looking for the patterns, reserving their attention for those higher-level issues which cut across departments and functions.

Converting problems into opportunities

Good managers have a way of converting problems into opportunities. Dealing with the troublesome problem of inventory costs getting out of control becomes an opportunity to introduce new procedures and new *thinking* into the whole logistics area. Having to solve the nagging problem of good sales performers leaving because they can earn substantially more with one of our competitors becomes an opportunity to put a tighter-knit, better-motivated team of sales people out in the field.

Calling it an 'opportunity' doesn't mean that we've solved the problem or made it any *easier* to solve the problem. What it does, though, is put a positive face on it. In many cases we've effectively taken a *Fix-It* type of problem and bolted a *Do-It* problem onto it.

It also makes the problem worth solving – if there was any doubt about that in the first place. You're not just putting out a fire. You're helping to build a better, more effective, more prosperous organisation. You're doing it by putting a better procedure in place, or by changing the way people *think* about the future growth of our business.

> What we've effectively done is taken a *Fix-It* type of problem and bolted a *Do-It* problem onto it.

Challenging others to do likewise

Linda, we've had a number of complaints from customers over the past three months about produce being shipped a day or two late. I'd like you to look into it and see what the problem is and what we can do about it.

That's straightforward enough. Linda, here's a practical problem which, because it involves customers, is important. Find out what's causing it and do whatever has to be done to make it go away.

Imagine how much more exciting it would be to add on the following:

> *I want our level of service to be a key selling feature all by itself. I want customers to absolutely rave about the way we treat them. Clearly, on the basis of what I've been hearing, we're not there yet. I'd like you to put together a strategy for making this a truly customer-driven organisation.*

Not just 'solve this problem' ... but *use* this problem as an *opportunity* to help us do something really exciting and critical to the business.

Summary

In this chapter we have looked at the role of you as a manager in the problem-solving process.

- If the whole thrust of your job is to have an impact on the way things are done by other people around you, then you are a 'manager'.
- *Leverage* allows us to wield an influence that extends further and deeper than anything we could produce if we were acting solely on our own.
- As managers, leverage is what we have to aim for. In everything we do.
- The *directive* approach to managing involves trying to be helpful by offering a solution to the problem – giving advice, for example.
- But there's no *leverage*. You haven't left the other person better equipped to solve the *next* problem.
- People learn best when they arrive at the solution themselves. Our job, as managers, is to help them do that.
- The *facilitative* approach to managing starts with an assumption – *Frank is capable of solving this problem; I don't have to solve it for him.*
- The skilful use of questions not only *activates* the person's thinking but actually *directs* it along lines which we know will be productive.

- As managers, we have to *invest* our time in those issues where our specific skills and insight will make a difference.
- The challenge is to bring our *usage* of time under our direct control – by making conscious, intelligent investment decisions.
- Reserve time for management by 'walking around'.
- Moving in and out of situations is an important managerial skill. Linger just along enough to make a *difference*.
- Look for opportunities to turn *Fix-It* problems into *Do-It* problems.

Just to get a handle
on a problem we
have to look at
how it is seen by
other people.

CHAPTER 14

Problem Solving *en Groupe*

I ncreasingly, in responding to today's problem-solving challenges, we have to harness the power of the group and indeed of the total organisation.

Rarely – these days – does a single person deal with a problem in isolation. More often than not a problem-solving effort involves quite a few different people both within and outside the organisation. Just to get a handle on a problem we have to look at how it is seen by a number of different people – each coming at it from their own unique vantage point.

The choices

Deciding when and how to use the resources of the group is not a simple case of yes or no. In practice, there is a range of options.

- *Individual process.* As the manager, we assess the problem and announce our solution to the group. That doesn't imply that we do it in an arbitrary fashion. Indeed, we do it positively – so that people understand why and how the decision was made.
- *Consultation.* We consult with the group – get their views, get a feel for which way people are leaning – but then make the final decision ourselves.
- *Group process.* The group solves the problem. As the manager, our task is to engineer the smooth sailing from initial debate to final decision. We abide by the group decision even if we don't agree with it.

The *individual* approach – where we mastermind the total problem-solving cycle – is clearly the best choice when:

- There is a tight deadline that has to be met.
- The issue under consideration is confidential.
- We are dealing with a crisis or emergency.

Or, indeed, when we – as manager – have a clear sense of where the group ought to be going and suspect that, left to their own resources, that's not at all where they would go.

The *group* approach, on the other hand, becomes essential when the enthusiastic commitment of each and every individual is vital to the success of our undertaking. Commitment flows from ownership, and ownership flows from involvement (Figure 29).

Fig. 29. Group commitment model.

That is, by now, a well-established fact that doesn't need a great deal of elaboration.

The *consultative* approach is useful when specialist input is required at some stage in the problem-solving cycle. We need to look at costs, for example, and we'll need to bring in someone who can help us through that area. The consultative approach is also useful when, to get to the bottom of the problem, we need to find out where and how various people on the team are being affected.

There are times, too, when it makes sense to use the *group* or *consultative* approach because of certain other benefits which they offer ...

The benefits of working together

Sheer productivity – measured in terms of the quantity and quality of ideas produced – tends to be higher in a group. With a variety of people around the table there is a deeper fund of material to draw upon.

Cross-fertilisation is another benefit. Jennifer's comment triggers a reaction from Frank. The presence of the two people from Marketing keeps the sales people on their toes.

Communication is a third benefit. People will know why a solution was arrived at and will work together to *implement* it because they worked together during the earlier phases of the problem-solving process.

Risk-taking is a fourth benefit. Studies have shown that groups are more likely to take risks than individuals acting alone. This might be because the pressure of individual accountability is removed and people feel freer to subscribe to a bolder course of action.

Leadership behaviours

There are *drawbacks* associated with the use of a *group* or *consultative* approach to problem-solving and the most obvious of these is inefficiency.

> *I hate meetings. I hate them intensely. They are a complete and utter waste of time. We sit and talk at each other. Most of what needs to be said doesn't get said because people are afraid to come right out and say what's on their mind. As a result, we end up agreeing to things that we don't really agree with, and we go away feeling worse than we did when we came in, and it spoils the whole bloody day unless you're lucky enough to have a pub lunch scheduled for right after the meeting.*

That is not an uncommon view of the way group meetings work. And the reason for that is a lack of effective *leadership*.

This is not the time to conduct a full-length workshop on the leadership of team meetings. But it might be helpful to at least list certain actions which help keep a group on track. They don't all have to be provided by you, the manager, but at various points in virtually any group meeting, *someone* will have to supply them.

Agenda setting

This means helping the group decide what to talk about – if only by offering a specific suggestion. *Why don't we start by defining what we mean by 'strategic'?*

Encouragement

Encouraging someone to speak up – specifically someone who seems to be reticent or shy or disinterested – is an important leadership behaviour.

Gate keeping

This means managing the flow of communications traffic. Making sure that everyone gets a chance to talk.

Policing

Stepping in or speaking up when someone else in the group is being disruptive or is dominating the discussion.

Reflection

This gives the speaker a chance to hear their thoughts expressed aloud and perhaps move beyond them.

If I understand you correctly, Linda, you think that it's the tone of his suggestion – not the content – which caused it to be rejected.

Re-focusing

Re-focusing means getting the discussion back on track – bringing the group back to the main issues – when it seems to be getting bogged down in details or tangential issues.

I think we're drifting away from the main issue here. We agreed that Step One was to define the problem, and I'm not sure that we've done that yet.

Topic changing

Initiating a change in topic. Suggesting that it is appropriate for the group to move on to another topic. It might involve suggesting that we leave this for now and talk about something else and then come back to this later.

Listen, why don't we spend a few minutes talking about the newsletter. Then we can break for coffee, relax a bit, and come back to this issue later.

Problem identification

This means explaining the reasons for a disagreement that the group itself is experiencing. I think we're talking about two different issues here.

The real key here is to identify the problem in process terms, so that it carries a suggestion of what can be done about it.

I think the reason we're having trouble making progress is that we haven't really agreed on just how broad our mandate is.

Summarising

It is very useful, as a means of moving things toward some sort of decision to periodically stop and summarise what has been said.

What we seem to be saying, as a group, is that we haven't been given enough information to make this type of decision.

Consensus testing

Issuing a trial balloon. This contributes quite directly to helping the group arrive at a decision or move ahead in the discussion.

Are we all agreed, then, that our mandate is to develop a list of options rather than actually make a decision?

The problem-solving team

Solving problems and making decisions isn't just an important part of a manager's day-to-day work. It is also something that he or she has to help *other* people do effectively. And we owe it to ourselves to step back and look at just how well our organisation promotes and nurtures its own problem-solving procedures.

Let's look at some of the relevant characteristics which we commonly find in high-performing teams and high-performing organisations.

1. People feel confident

In the right environment, under the right manager where problem-solving *effectiveness* has taken hold, the shy person is a bit less shy and less tentative, the hesitant decision-maker is a bit more assured and purposeful.

People feel good about themselves. They have learned through experience that their ideas count, that their opinions will be listened to. They aren't under pressure to justify everything they want to do or get approval for every little decision they have to make.

2. They have a sense of mission

In the problem-solving organisation, people have a sense of purpose and mission. They are not simply coming in every day to do their jobs. They work for an organisation that is helping to create and satisfy an important need in the marketplace:

- We are making the world's finest wristwatches.
- We are making it safer for women to have babies.
- We are developing a cure for lymphoma.
- We are changing people's eating habits.

You quickly get a sense that people are working together toward a common end. That doesn't mean that people don't argue or come into conflict; but the arguments and conflicts are *meaningful* ones that have to do with important ends and strategies rather than reflecting petty differences or territorial disputes. There is, too, a *can-do* feeling that may even spill into cockiness at times. People know that what they're doing is important.

3. People are pushing for results

You would think that pushing for results ought to be the norm, in every organisation. But it's not. Scratch the average worker deep enough and you will find that their real concern is with doing a good job. Is that not the same as pushing for results? No, it's not. Doing a good job means striving for the recognition that a person rightly gets for having a good attitude and putting in a heartfelt effort.

But it's not the same as pushing for results.

The person who pushes for results is truly not satisfied until *results* are produced ... until the customer's problem has been solved, until the decision has been made.

4. *They have the freedom to make mistakes*

People aren't jumped upon if they make a mistake, nor is the climate one in which people avoid mistakes by erring consistently on the side of safety and prudence. No, the key thing is that people recognise that making mistakes is part of the learning process.

Here's Tony Martindale again:

'Sometimes we forget how eager we were to try out our new ideas. All our people, I'm sure, have new ideas, too. They're itching to take a crack at putting them into practice, to swim in a little deeper water and justify their membership on the team. Good. You give them the chance. But maybe the idea doesn't work out quite so well. If there's a reprimand, what happens? Every time that enterprising spirit is broken down even a little, every time that little spark of originality is snuffled out, we are choking off the very tap-roots of our organisation's precious fund of creativity.'

5. *There is a sense of urgency in the air*

When you watch a high-performing team in action, you rarely get a sense that you are looking at a relaxed, laid-back group of people. There is a charge in the air, a buzz, a sense that important things are being decided and accomplished. There is a sense that time is of the essence, that we have to move *quickly* on things.

6. *People sort problems out themselves*

People don't run to their superiors every time they have a problem. They sort it out amongst themselves.

If there's a problem that has to do with shipping, then I can usually get it sorted out by going directly to Jim. He and I came up through the ranks together and we seem to have a fairly good understanding. And then, once a month or so, we sit down and look at where we can save time by getting our two departments to work more closely together. It's amazing how many little things end up wasting time just because no one has ever taken the time to look at them.

7. *Communication is direct and non-stop*

People communicate face-to-face rather than relying on formal channels. Meetings are brief and productive, and kept to a minimum. The telephone lines are in constant use. Brief e-mail messages take the place of lengthy letters and proposals. Computers are linked so that everyone has access to the same data and can see at a glance what is happening in other segments of the business.

8. *Conflict is dealt with constructively*

Conflicts are put to good use, used in a positive way to help the team move forward.

A healthy team will not shy away from conflict that involves substantive *ideas*. Indeed, top-performing teams seem to recognise that a certain level of conflict is both inevitable and desirable. It demonstrates that the quality of communication is honest and candid, and that debate is not being cut off prematurely in the dubious interests of harmony or team spirit.

Likewise, managers aren't hesitant to clamp down on someone who has made a careless mistake or failed to deliver a promised result on time. But it's done constructively. It's an honest expression of concern, accompanied by an equally genuine shifting of attention to how we can prevent the problem from happening again.

9. *Systems are results-driven*

In an effective problem-solving organisation, there is a disciplined emphasis on goals and performance, and part of this is a belief in doing things systematically and measuring results. But systems are not allowed to become ends in themselves. They serve as a vehicle for reaching goals. They enable work to move forward with maximum speed and efficiency. The minute they stop doing that, they are changed or removed or otherwise got out of the way.

Here's Graeme Weir again:

> 'There are some key numbers that we all have to know about because they tell us where we are going. There are certain rules we all follow because then we don't go around tripping over one

another's toes. There are certain policies that we all know have to be adhered to because they represent our commitment to a certain way of doing business. And then there are certain procedures and systems that we all use because they make life easier; they allow us to get things done faster and with less fuss and bother. But that's it. Beyond that, there aren't too many times during the day when you'll find someone doing something a certain way just because it's "supposed to be done that way." We expect people to think.'

10. The team possesses 'self-belief'

There is a belief that the team is capable of dealing with things. There is a willingness to tackle problems head-on, to put issues out on the table, to be brutally objective about customer perceptions and market strengths, to use language that reflects the *reality* of things rather than an image that the organisation is straining to project. People aren't defensive. They aren't afraid to really *dig into* issues and get at the truth of what is happening.

Creating the right climate

It has often been said that a company gets the front-line problem-solving effectiveness that it deserves. In other words, it won't get a lot of people demonstrating innovative spirit and decisiveness unless a climate capable of *nurturing* such qualities has been created.

The question is this. Do we, as a company, make it easy for people to be effective problem-solvers? Or, are we inadvertently making it difficult for them to unleash their talents?

To answer that, we need to know what specific *organisational* things work for and against effective problem-solving.

In Figure 30 we have a brief listing of elements which work for – or against – the creation of an effective problem-solving climate. The condition described in the left-hand column works *for* problem-solving effectiveness. The condition described in the right-hand column works *against* it.

Adapting to a No-No-No-No environment

Of the fifteen items included in Figure 30, the following are especially important. They tell us whether the culture of our

1. Intelligent risk-taking is encouraged.	Y ☐ ☐ N
People are encouraged to think boldly about things and take intelligent risks.	People learn quickly that it is better to err on the side of safety and caution.

2. New ideas are encouraged.	Y ☐ ☐ N
People are encouraged to come forward with new ideas and proposals.	People who try to put forth new ideas just end up feeling frustrated.

3. Mistakes are tolerated	Y ☐ ☐ N
An honest mistake is tolerated, so long as you learn something from it.	Managers tend to come down hard on someone who has made a mistake.

4. There is room for initiative.	Y ☐ ☐ N
People are given lots of room to think for themselves and exercise initiative.	People are expected to follow rules and stay within the boundary lines of their job.

5. We communicate.	Y ☐ ☐ N
Communication is direct, immediate, and honest. We *talk* to one another.	There is too much reliance on formal channels, too much rumour and gossip.

6. Senior managers are in touch.	Y ☐ ☐ N
Senior managers have a good feel for what is happening at the lower levels.	Senior management is out of touch with the everyday reality of the organisation.

7. Financial results are shared.	Y ☐ ☐ N
People are kept well informed of the group's financial results. Nothing is hidden.	Information is shared on a need-to-know basis. Secrecy and confusion abound.

8. The overall direction is clear.	Y ☐ ☐ N
The mission is clear. The priorities are identified. People know what has to be done.	We don't have a tangible, coherent sense of direction for the team as a whole.

9. Accountabilities are clear.	Y ☐ ☐ N
Outcomes are tied to specific people. People know who is accountable for what.	Accountabilities are fuzzy, and there is lots of room for people to 'escape'.

Fig. 30. The problem-solving environment.

10. Performance problems are tackled head-on.	Y ☐ ☐ N
Performance problems are dealt with in an immediate and above-board fashion.	Performance problems tend to be swept under the rug and allowed to linger on.

11. There is a sense of teamwork.	Y ☐ ☐ N
There is a sense of us all pulling together in a common direction.	There is little sense of us all pulling together toward a common objective.

12. We're flexible.	Y ☐ ☐ N
We can get the right people dealing with the right problem at the right time.	Too often, our organisational structure hinders rather than facilitates problem-solving.

13. Decision-making is pushed down the ladder.	Y ☐ ☐ N
When a decision needs to be made, it gets made. One thing we *don't* do is pass the buck.	It's difficult to get a decision made. No one seems to want to step up to bat.

14. Decisions get made quickly.	Y ☐ ☐ N
Decision-making tends to be pushed down the ladder as far as possible.	Key decisions tend to be made by a select group at the top of the organisation.

15. We are customer-oriented.	Y ☐ ☐ N
It's just not an empty slogan. This is truly a customer-driven organisation.	We *say* we are customer-driven, but it's not reflected in our day-to-day practises.

Fig. 30 – continued.

organisation is going to make it easy or difficult for us to be effective problem-solvers:

♦ Intelligent risk-taking is encouraged.
♦ New ideas are encouraged.
♦ Mistakes are tolerated.
♦ There is room for initiative.

If an honest look around our own company tells us that we're working in a *No-No-No-No* environment, then we either have to leave or adapt. It is unlikely, unless we own or run the business, that we can do much to *change* the environment.

> If an honest look around our own company tells us that we're working in a *No-No-No-No* environment, then we either have to leave or adapt.

Adapting means you require a good deal of maturity and patience. For one thing, you have to be willing to settle for something less than you had originally hoped for. Rather than urging the committee to accept the innovative proposal that you think is needed you have to scale it down a bit and factor out some of the risks. That makes it a bit less exciting, a bit less *avant garde* – but it also gives it a fighting chance of being accepted.

Adapting means recognising and accepting the need to rally support behind the scenes, sound out key influencers in advance of decisions being tabled, take extra time to present your ideas in the right light and with the right back-up, and so on ... all of which demand time and energy which could be much more profitably spent on other things.

Adapting means you have to decide where to take a stand and where to let something go. That means, amongst other things, learning to live with a certain amount of imperfection. If you're a perfectionist, or an idealist, or a self-styled radical, then you're in the wrong environment.

Adapting means biting your tongue from time to time. You have to watch what you say and how you say it and to *whom* you say it and *when* you say it. It sounds like a small thing, but it's not. Not being able to say out loud what is on your mind is an insidious form of pressure and takes its toll on a person. Once we get to the point where the only time we can talk freely is in the loo or over lunch in the pub down he street, then it becomes very, very difficult to really enjoy the work we do. Freedom of speed isn't just a constitutional right. It's one of the real underpinnings of job satisfaction.

Climate surveys

The utility of a list such as the one in Figure 30 is demonstrated when we build it into a *climate survey*. Properly designed and administered, a climate survey affords us a unique opportunity to see ourselves, as an organisation, through the eyes of our people.

It highlights the differences in perception that exist between rank-and-file employees and senior managers. And – if there are specific things that we, as a company or as a senior management team, are doing that get in the *way* of people giving us their best performance – then a well-designed survey ought to get those things right out on the table where we can decide what action to take.

Hiring problem-solving talent

One way to foster effective problem-solving throughout the entire organisation is to place a clear emphasis on problem-solving *skills* and *talent* when we hire people or consider moving them into positions of greater responsibility.

Although this seems like an obvious strategy, not many companies really do a good job on this front. We pay a lot of attention to qualifications, technical skills and background, and we do our best to evaluate such personality traits as enthusiasm, ambition and willingness to work hard. And our judgement is certainly influenced by the poise, self-assurance and communication skills a job candidate displays during an interview.

But there are at least *six* specific qualities – very relevant to the solving of problems – which we aren't very good at assessing:

- *Critical thinking.* Is this a person who will think critically about the way things are, challenge the comfortable assumptions that people are making, question conventional wisdom?
- *Incisiveness.* How skilful is this person at seeing what the real issues are in a complex situation, separating what *counts* in a situation from what is not so important?
- *Analytical skill.* Is the person good at *straight* thinking – asking the right questions in the right order, not looking for solutions or trying to move into action before the problem has been properly defined?
- *Judgement.* Are the person's analytical skills and technical knowledge blended with good judgement, good business sense, commercial awareness, *common* sense, a willingness to rely on intuition when necessary?
- *Action orientation.* Is this someone who will act decisively, move from analysis to action at the earliest possible

opportunity, and bring a sense of *urgency* into a problem-solving situation?

♦ *Leadership.* Can they lead the way forward towards the solution, mobilising and energising other people, giving them a vision of the result we are after and a sense of confidence about us being able to get there?

For the most part, the assessment of job candidates is still a primitive art. Most large companies still rely heavily on some combination of the traditional interview and personnel testing, and smaller firms often rely on the interview alone.

Sound hiring doesn't necessarily require a lot of fancy or elaborate techniques. Indeed, common sense is often our best guide of what to assess in a candidate and how to assess it. The people at Microsoft, for example, give a candidate a half-hour or

> The assessment of job candiates is still a primitive art.

so during the morning to look through a file outlining a problem, and then they grill them on it at some point during the afternoon. It's a good, quick, practical test of the candidate's problem-solving ability and presentation skills.

Setting a personal example

> Perhaps the best way to encourage other people to be effective problem-solvers is to give them a good model to emulate.

If you as a manager and role model for the people around you step in and do people's thinking for them, jump too quickly on people when they have made an honest mistake, close your mind to ideas which conflict with your own way of seeing things when there might be something there to build upon, you're setting the wrong example.

Here are the things you want to be able to say about yourself:

♦ I'm willing to tolerate an honest mistake so long as the other person has learned something from it.

♦ I expect people to act independently and display initiative, and they know that.

- I actively encourage people to think boldly, to experiment, to *challenge* conventional wisdom.
- I have introduced brainstorming as a way to help the team think creatively about things.
- I don't want people agreeing with everything I say. If they don't agree with something, I want to hear about it.
- I am willing to change my mind on a key issue if someone can give me a logical reason for doing so.
- I try to help people think things through rather than just giving them advice or telling them what to do.

And …

- People know these things about me.
- I've demonstrated them time and time again.

Summary

In this, the last chapter, we have looked at harnessing the powers of the group as part of the problem-solving process.

- Rarely – these days – does a single person deal with a problem in isolation. More often than not, problem-solving involves quite a few different people.
- Deciding when and how to use the resources of the group is not a simple case of yes or no. In practice, there is a range of options.
- An *individual* approach works best when there is a tight deadline that has to be met, the issue is confidential or we are dealing with a crisis.
- The *group* approach is essential when the enthusiastic commitment of each and every individual is vital to the success of our undertaking.
- The *consultative* approach is useful when specialist input is required or when we need to find out how various people are being affected.
- Generation of ideas, cross-fertilisation, communication, and risk-taking are four of the benefits from using a *consultative* or *group* approach.
- The biggest *drawback* in using a group approach is its inefficiency, and the single biggest cause of inefficiency is a lack of effective *leadership*.

- There are 10 characteristics that we see in high-performing teams and organisations – reflecting a high level of problem-solving effectiveness.
- Organisational *climate* can either nurture – or dampen – the initiative and resourcefulness with which people tackle problems.
- So, too, can the personal example that each and every manager sets for their people. We have to give them a model that they can emulate.

Recommended Reading

- Henry, Jane (Ed.), *Creative Management*, London: SAGE Publications, 1991.
- Loehle, Craig, *Thinking Strategically*, Cambridge: Cambridge University Press, 1996.
- Senge, Peter M., *The Fifth Discipline*, New York: Doubleday/Currency, 1990.
- Sternberg, Robert J., *Successful Intelligence*, New York: Simon & Schuster, 1996.

And the best reading material of all ... the business section of the *Times* or one of the other major London broadsheets. There is no better way to learn about problem-solving than to keep abreast of what real people and real companies are doing to meet the enormous challenges of doing business in today's volatile and brutally competitive environment.

Index